Northwest Lighthouses

A Coloring Collection

Volume 1

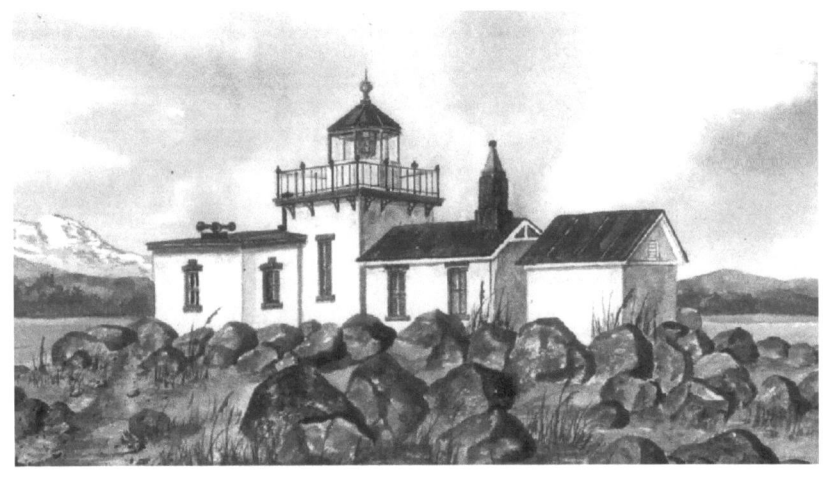

created by

Olivia Jane Williams

ojwilliams.39@gmail.com

www.oliviajanewilliams.com

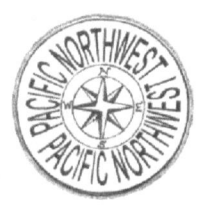

ISBN-13: 978-1535543194

ISBN-10:1535543191

O' sparkling jewel in lantern's crown
You guide the mariner's way
Across the boundless, rolling deep
A light thru night till dawning day.

JAG

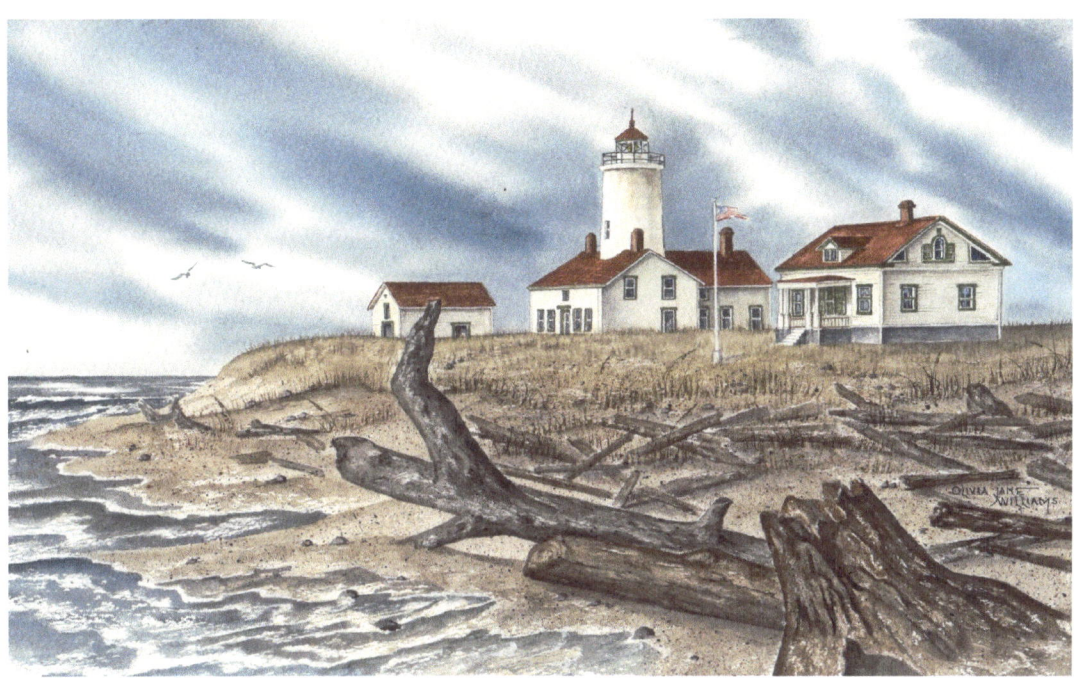

This book is dedicated to all the men and women who served as lighthouse keepers and kept the light burning to guide ships, attract commerce, and save lives.

Lighthouses are a unique expression of human creativity and engineering skill. Each stands as a solitary monument to the dedicated keepers who worked to safeguard marniers for more than two centuries.

In 1939, the U.S. Coast Guard was appointed 'guardian of the lights', and the task of lighting became automated. Since then, many lighthouses have become relics, for lack of maintence, and some have lost the 'jewel in their crowns'.

Lighthouses have always been a facination of mine. The sense of history and mystique they convey spans space and time. These sentinels are gifts of our heritage and should be perserved and passed on.

In 1996, I began painting Northwest lighthouses in watercolor. My realistic style allows me to produce an historical document of the unique architecture and setting of each one. Visiting them permits me to sense and see first hand their individual characters and incorporate this into the painting.

This book was created for you. Enjoy!

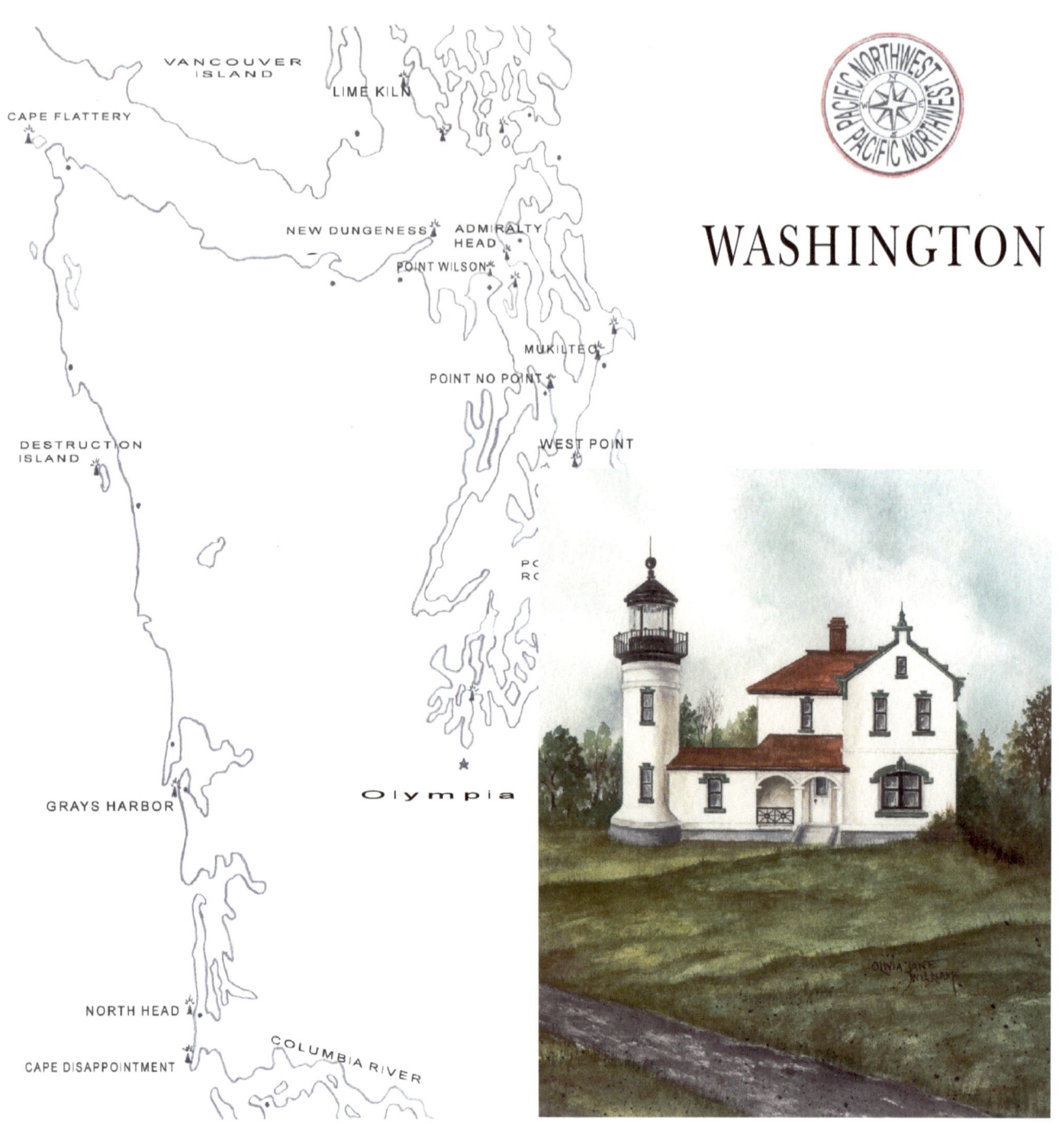

WASHINGTON

VANCOUVER ISLAND

LIME KILN

CAPE FLATTERY

NEW DUNGENESS
ADMIRALTY HEAD
POINT WILSON

MUKILTEO

POINT NO POINT

WEST POINT

DESTRUCTION ISLAND

Olympia

GRAYS HARBOR

NORTH HEAD

CAPE DISAPPOINTMENT

COLUMBIA RIVER

ADMIRALTY HEAD LIGHTHOUSE, built in 1903, replaced the original frame structure, which stood in the way of a planned gun placement at Fort Casey. The current masonry tower housed a fourth-order Fresnel lens, which was moved to the Dungeness Spit lighthouse in 1927 when shipping routes changed and made the light obsolete. The station dwelling became an Army officer's residence. The lighthouse is now a museum and a tourist attraction of Fort Casey State Park on Whidbey Island.

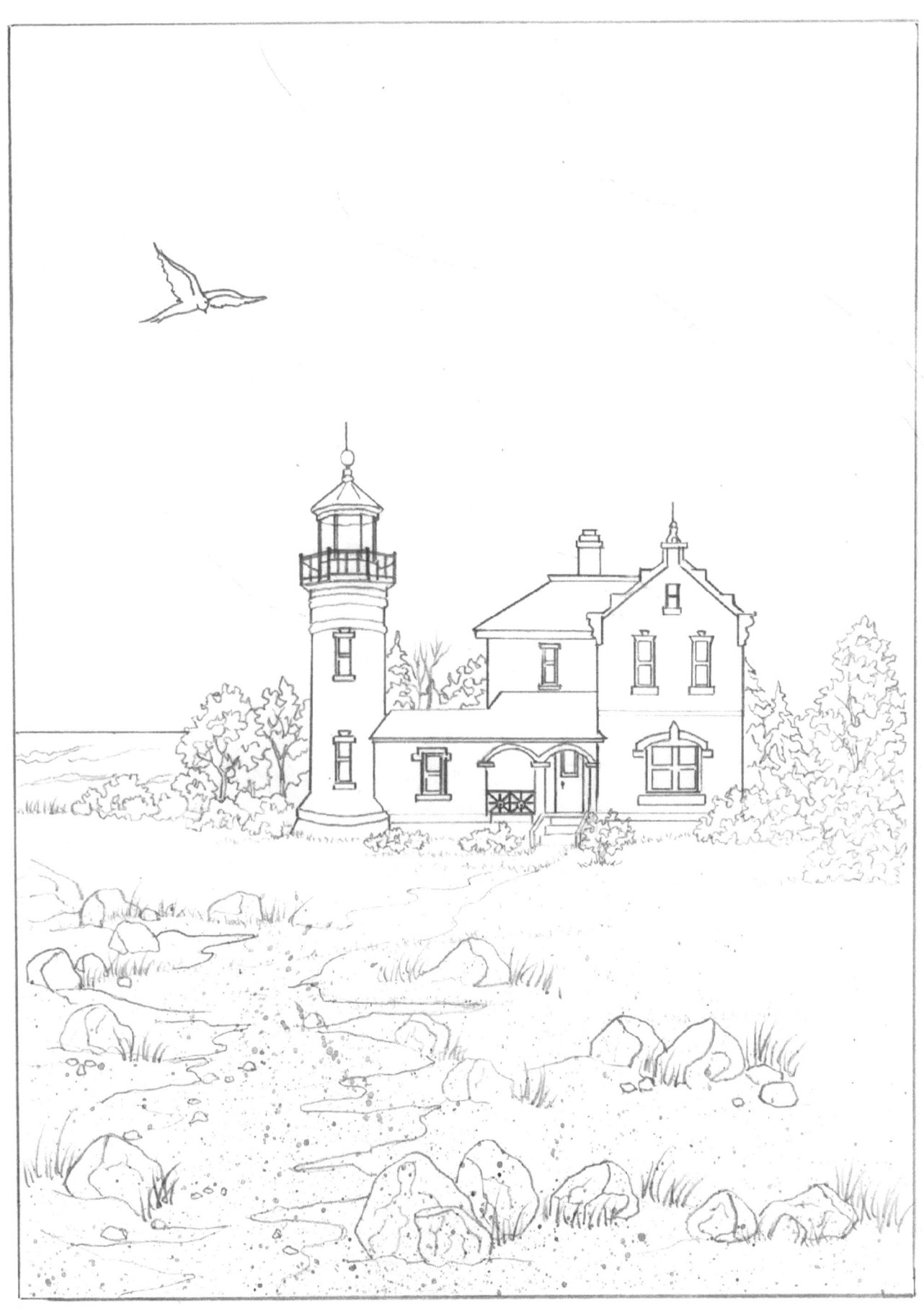

ADMIRALTY HEAD · Coupeville, WA

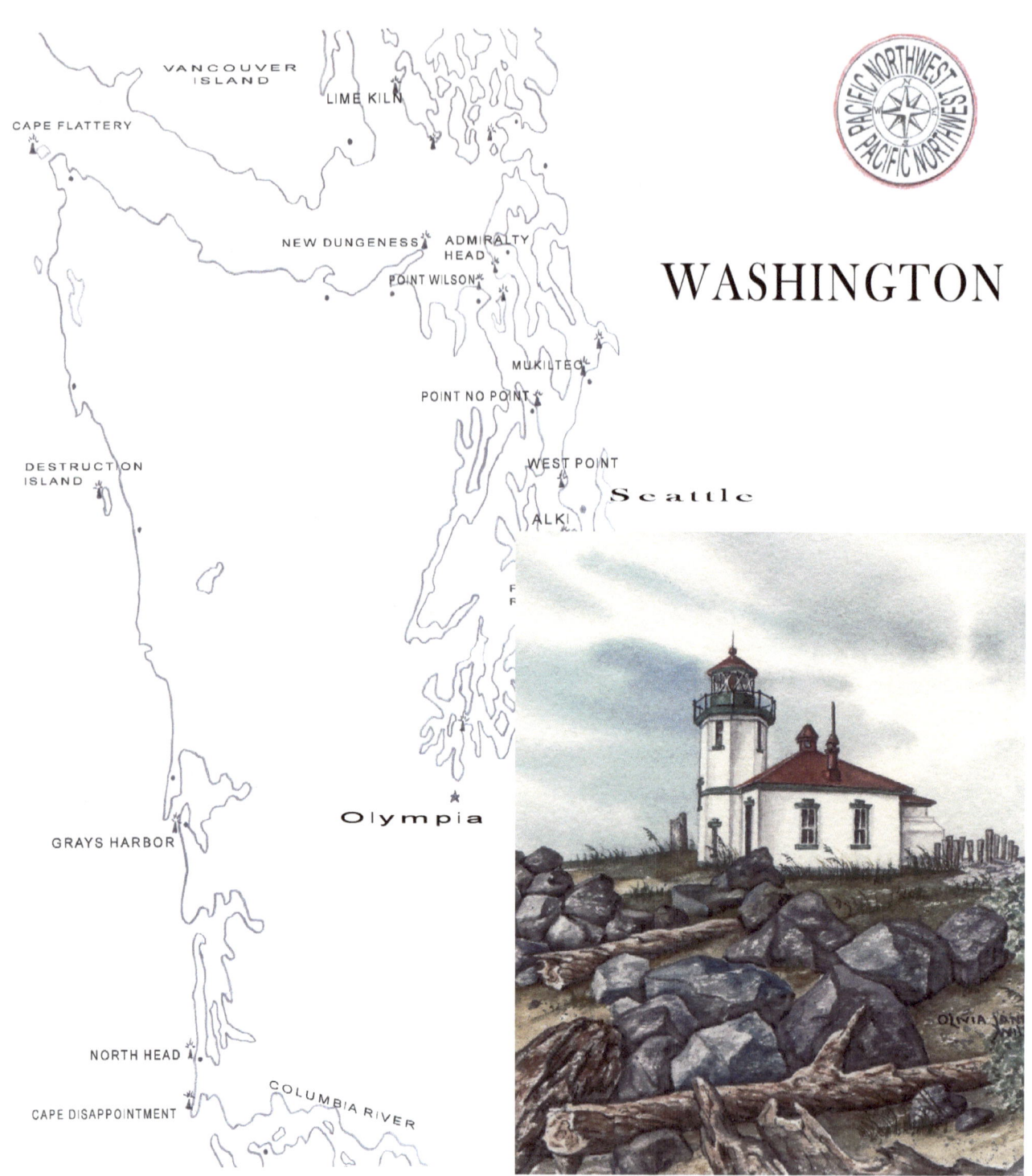

WASHINGTON

CAPE FLATTERY

VANCOUVER ISLAND

LIME KILN

NEW DUNGENESS

ADMIRALTY HEAD

POINT WILSON

MUKILTEO

POINT NO POINT

DESTRUCTION ISLAND

WEST POINT

Seattle

ALKI

Olympia

GRAYS HARBOR

NORTH HEAD

CAPE DISAPPOINTMENT

COLUMBIA RIVER

ALKI POINT LIGHTHOUSE, completed in 1918, stands at the south entrance to Seattle's Elliott Bay. The original lens was replaced by a modern apparatus, and a special direction-finder calibration service was added to the thirty-seven foot octagonal tower. With commerce increasing between Seattle and Tacoma, the lighthouse became a critical aid to navigation.

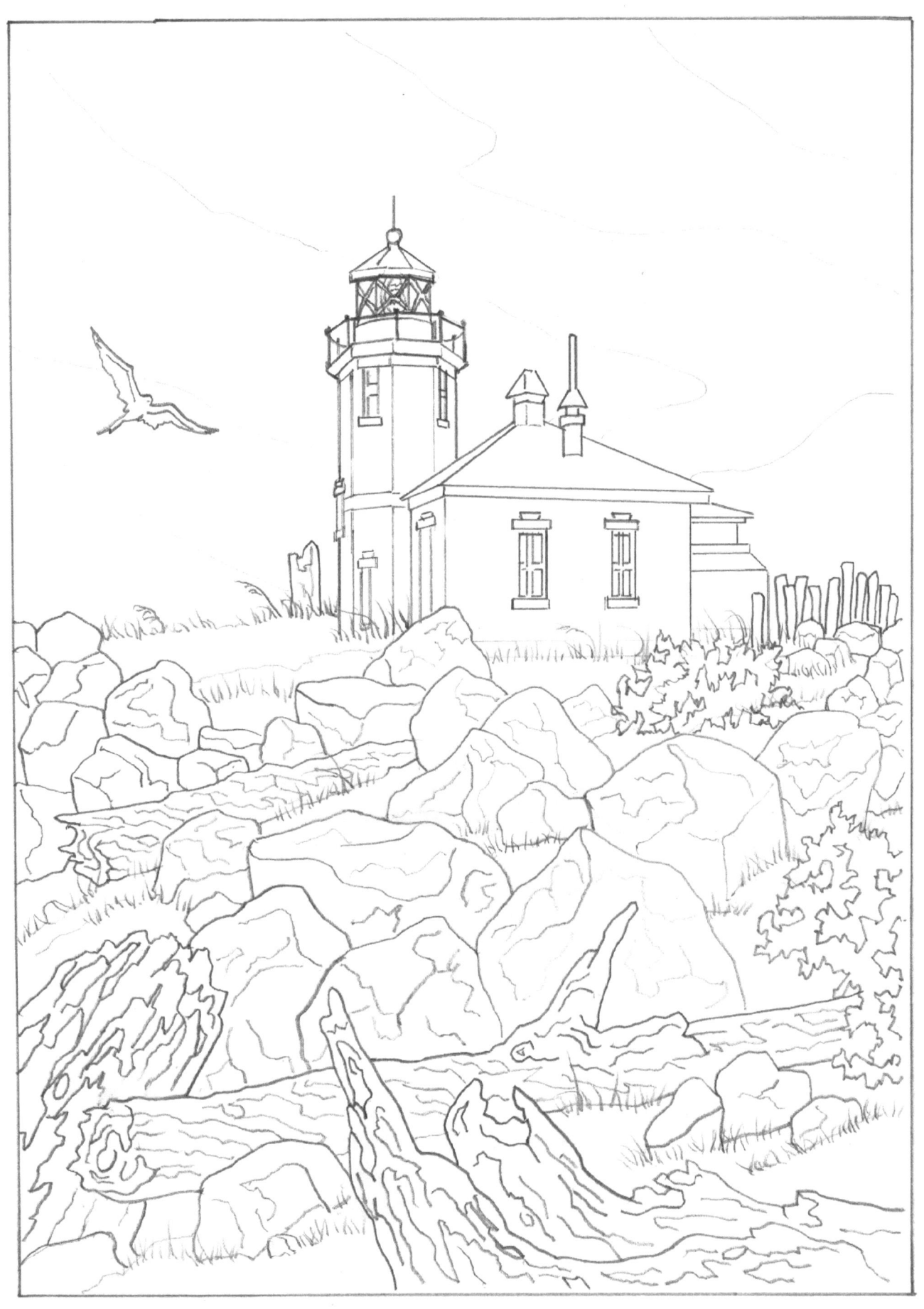

ALKI POINT - Seattle, WA

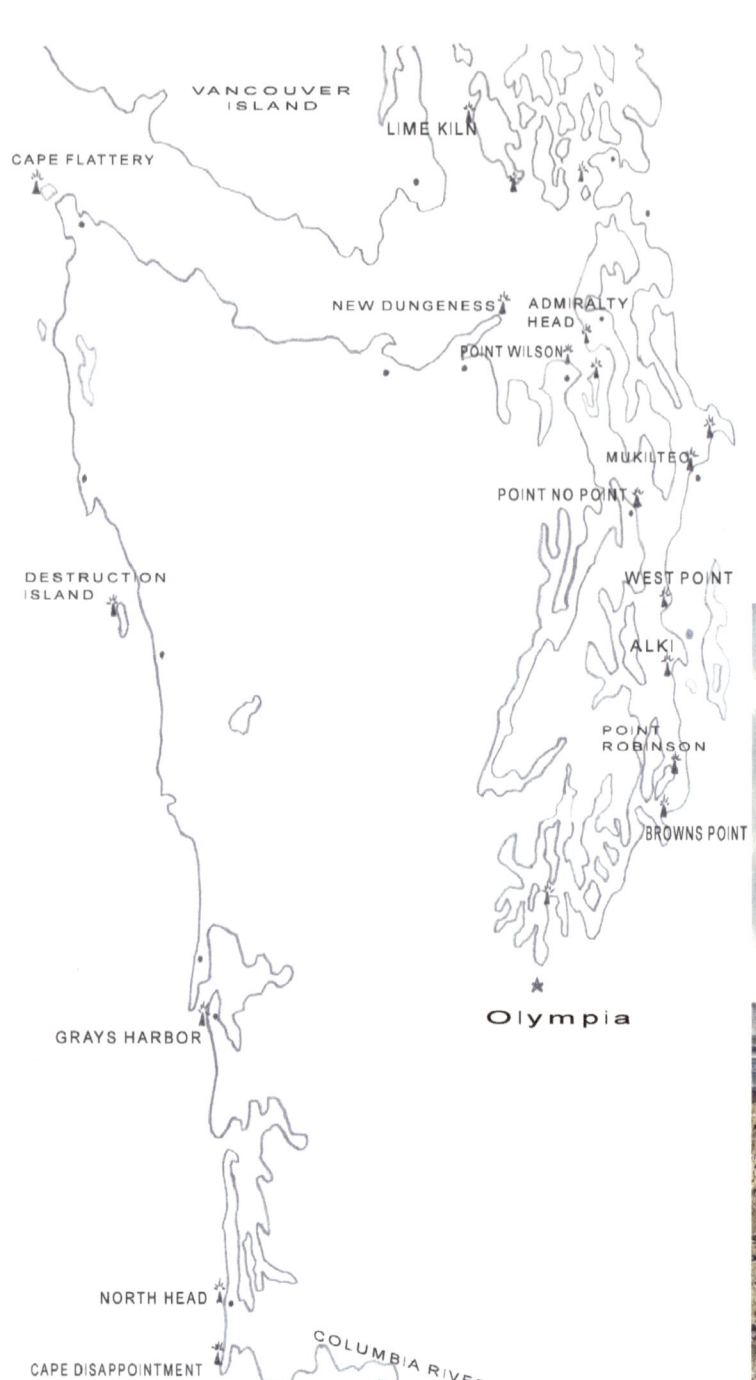

CAPE FLATTERY

VANCOUVER
ISLAND

LIME KILN

NEW DUNGENESS
ADMIRALTY
HEAD

POINT WILSON

MUKILTEO

POINT NO POINT

DESTRUCTION
ISLAND

WEST POINT

ALKI

POINT
ROBINSON

BROWNS POINT

GRAYS HARBOR

Olympia

NORTH HEAD

COLUMBIA RIVER

CAPE DISAPPOINTMENT

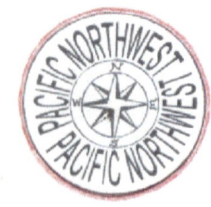

WASHINGTON

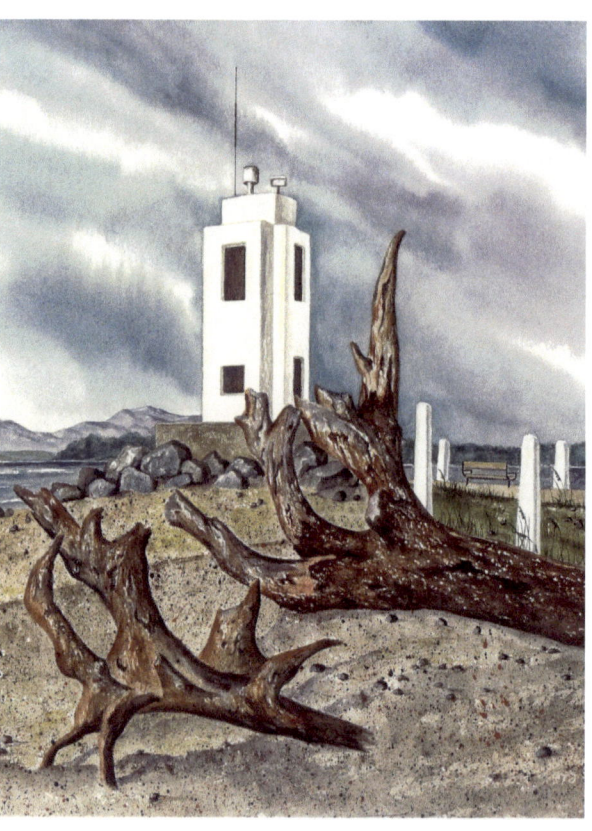

BROWNS POINT LIGHT was erected in 1933 to replace the original light and fog signal. It's thirty-one foot concrete tower sits at the west end of the entrance to Tacoma's Commencement Bay, a heavily traveled waterway for both commercial craft and private boaters. The beacon light is the guardian of Port Tacoma's sea lanes. Today the station remains an outstanding place to watch tug boats and deep sea ships entering the busy portal.

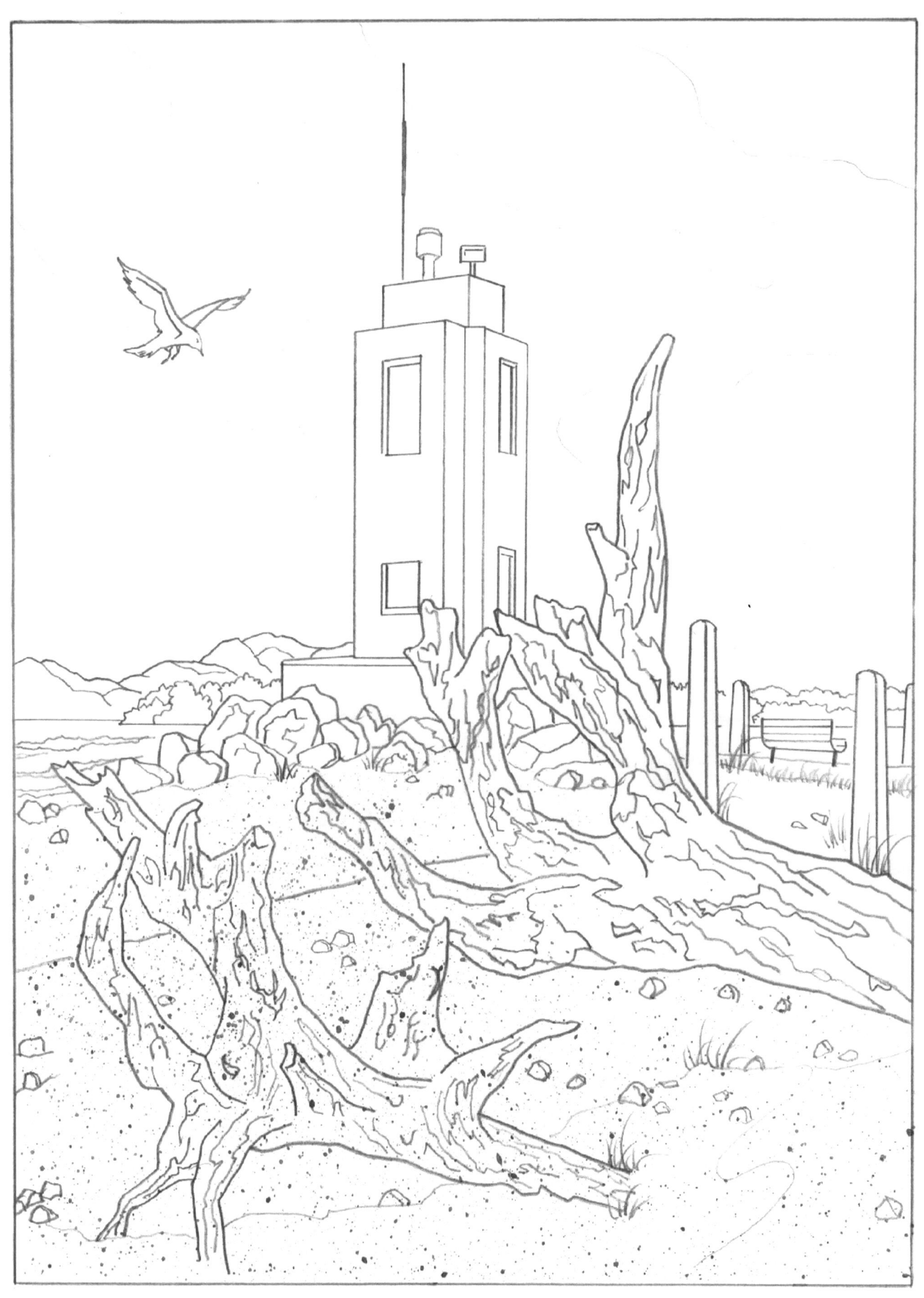

BROWNS POINT - Tacoma, WA

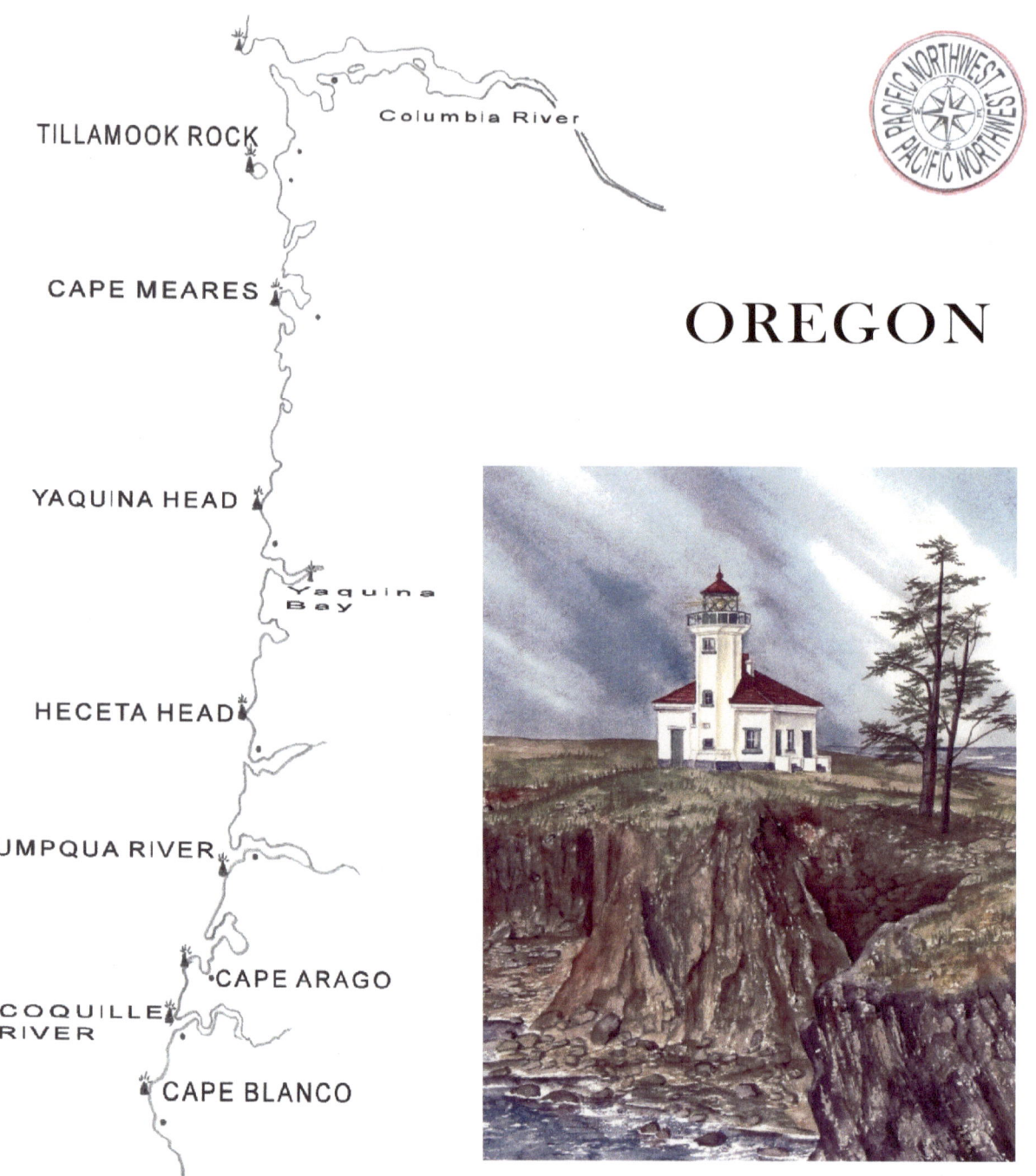

TILLAMOOK ROCK

Columbia River

CAPE MEARES

YAQUINA HEAD

Yaquina Bay

HECETA HEAD

UMPQUA RIVER

CAPE ARAGO

COQUILLE RIVER

CAPE BLANCO

OREGON

CAPE ARAGO LIGHTHOUSE located south of Coos Bay, is the third structure built on an island which is connected to the mainland by an iron footbridge. Completed in 1934, the octagonal tower of reinforced concrete stands forty-four feet tall and has a fourth-order light which is visible from sixteen miles at sea.

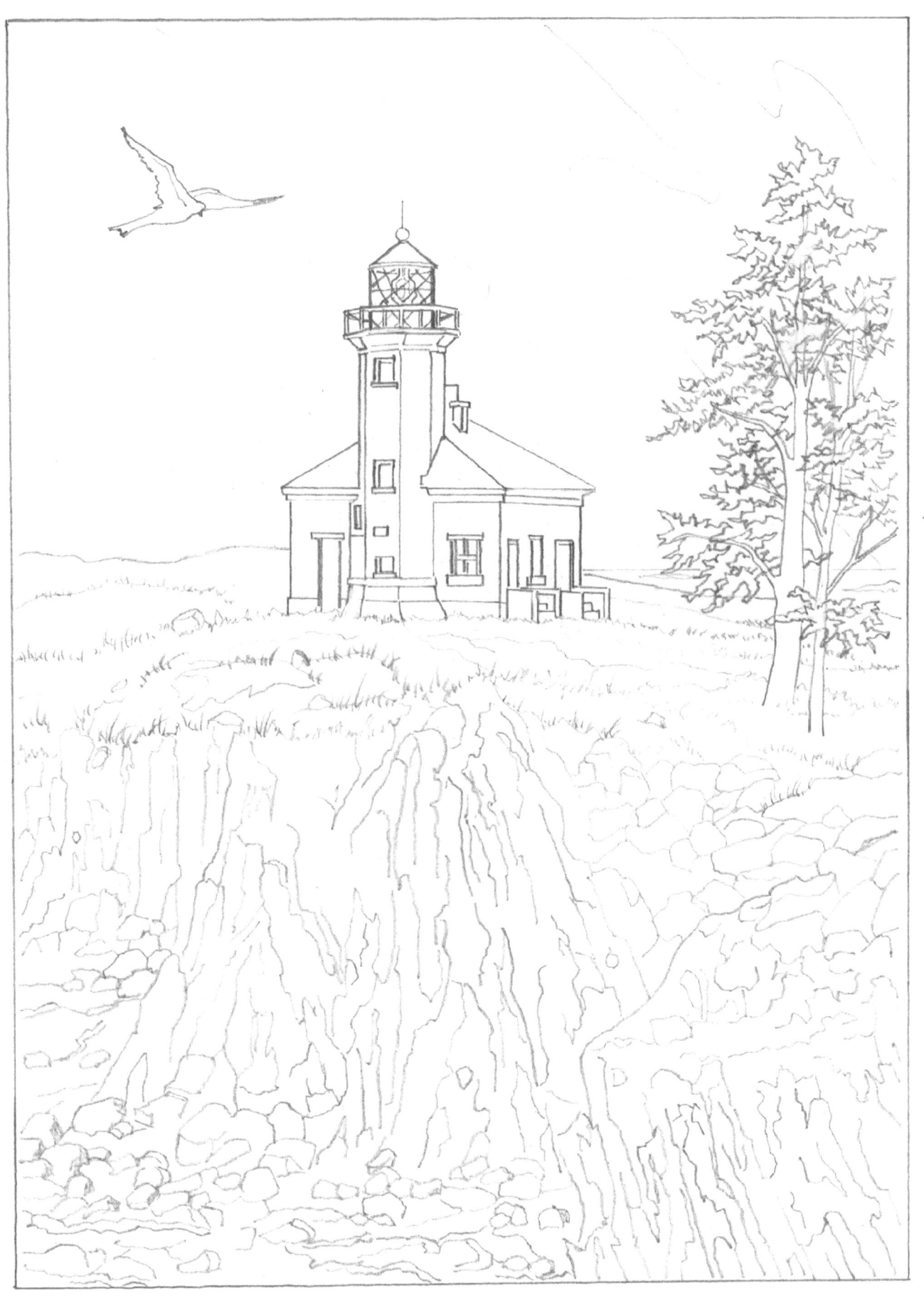

CAPE ARAGO - Coos Bay, OR

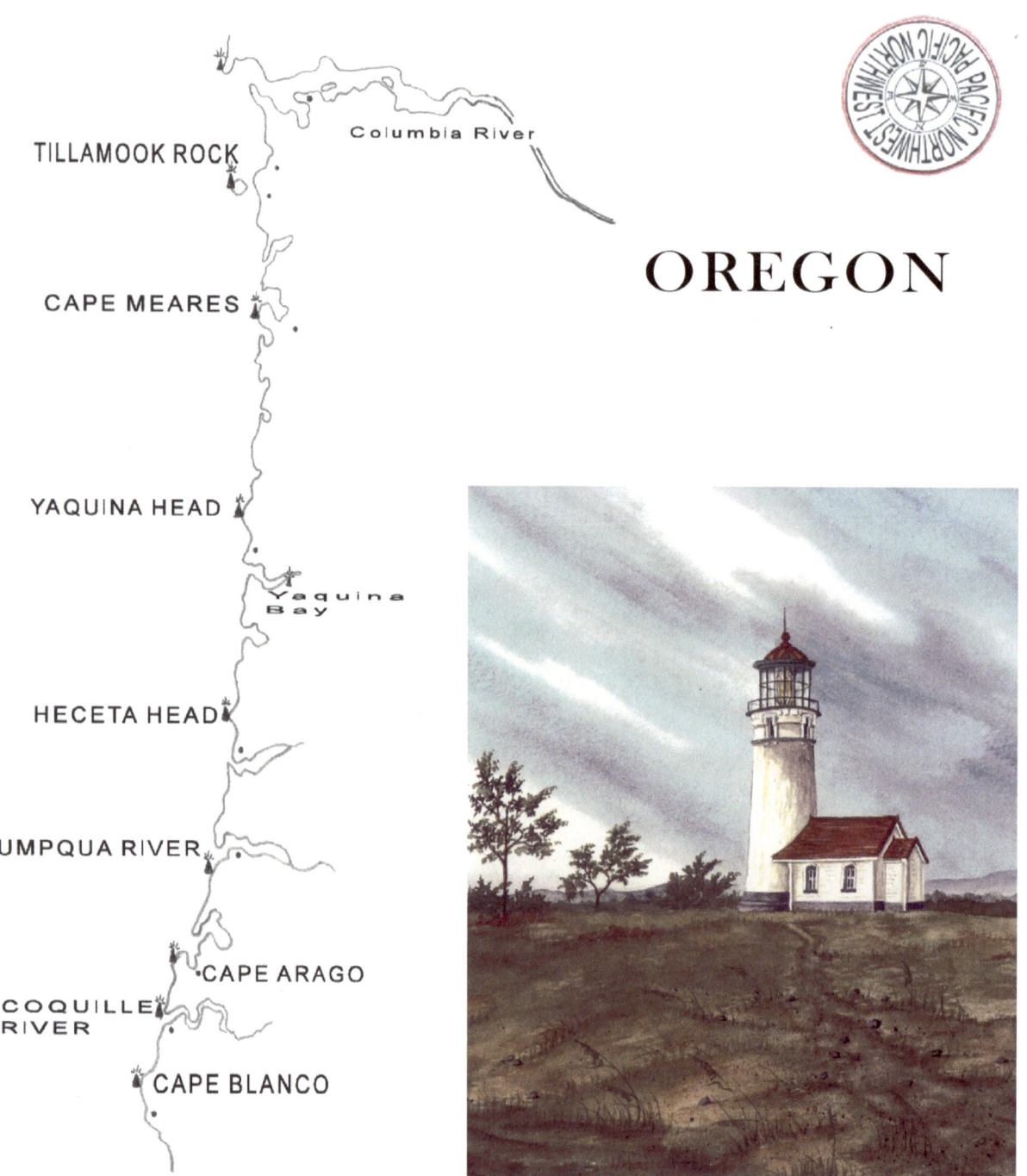

TILLAMOOK ROCK

Columbia River

CAPE MEARES

OREGON

YAQUINA HEAD

Yaquina Bay

HECETA HEAD

UMPQUA RIVER

CAPE ARAGO

COQUILLE RIVER

CAPE BLANCO

CAPE BLANCO LIGHTHOUSE, completed in 1870 and located near Port Orford, is Oregon's tallest lighthouse. The fifty-nine foot conical-shaped tower houses a second-order Fresnel lens. Rising 245 Feet above sea level, the light can be seen from twenty-two miles at sea.

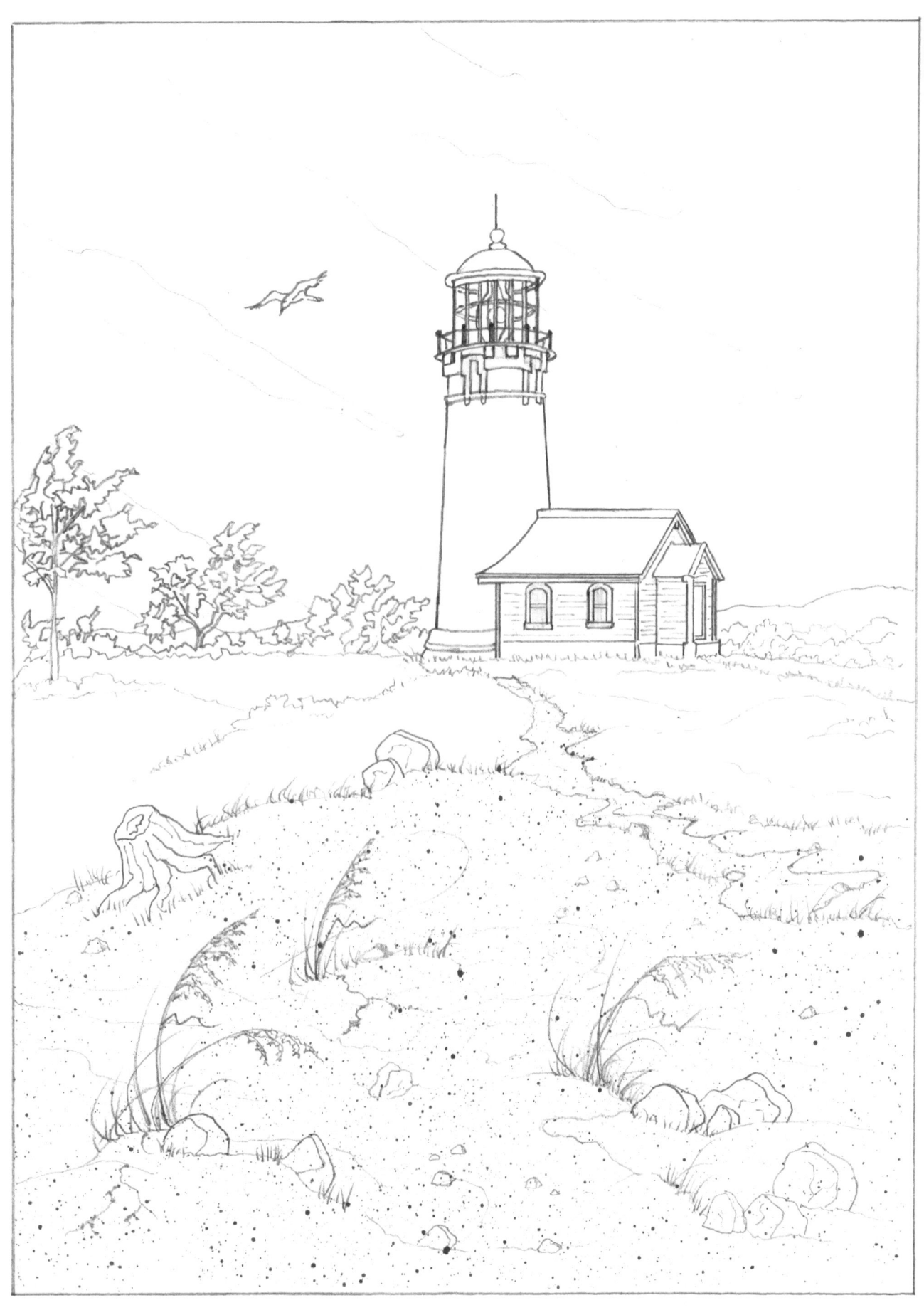

CAPE BLANCO, Port Orford, OR

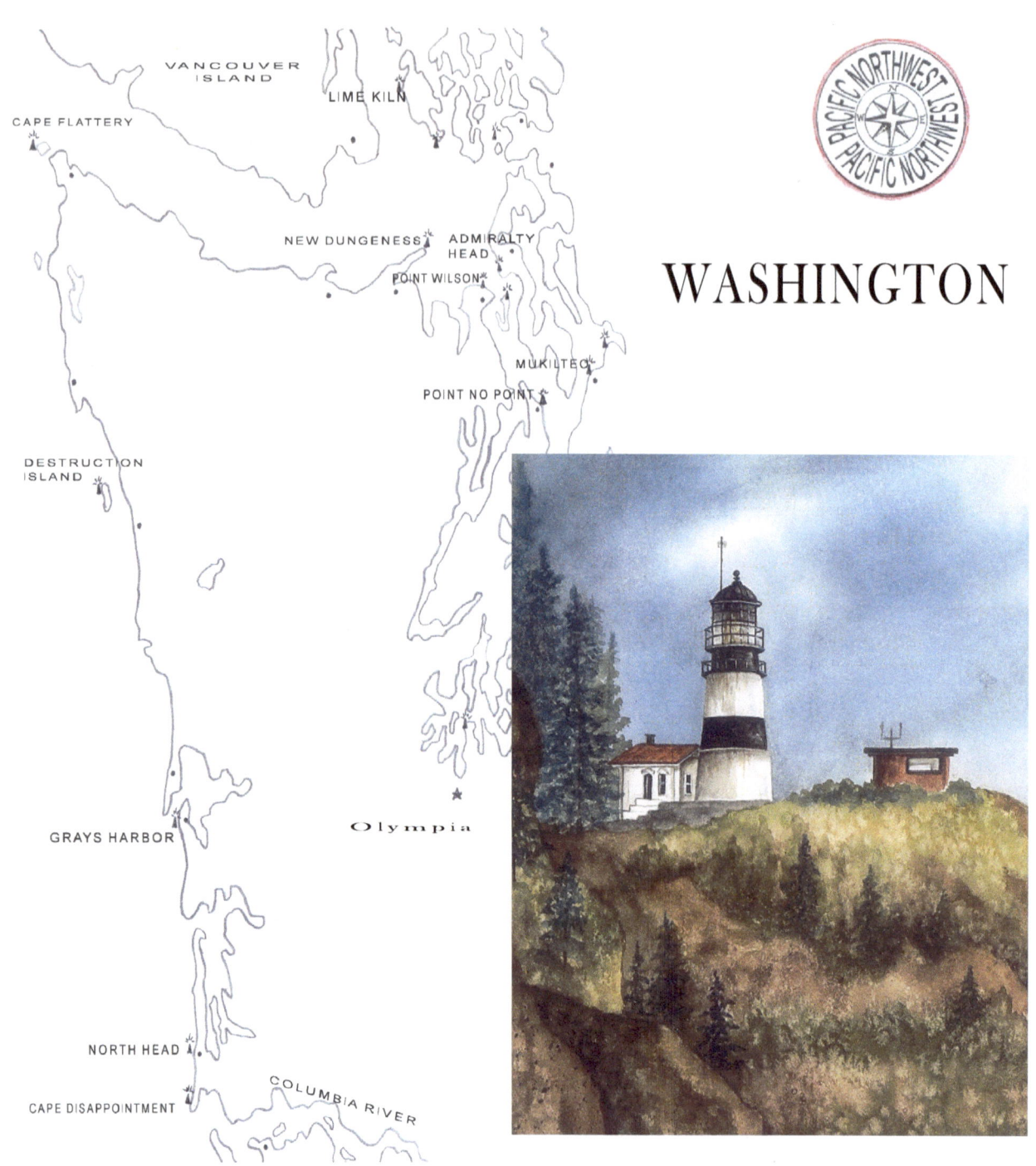

WASHINGTON

CAPE DISAPPOINTMENT LIGHTHOUSE, the oldest in the state, located near Ilwaco, Washington was given a first order Fresnel lens and lit on October 15, 1836. At a cost of $38,500, it was considered extraordinarily expensive. The fifty-three foot tower overlooks the meeting place of the Columbia River and the Pacific Ocean. Many vessels have met their destruction on or near this stony cape call "Disappointment". In 1864, Fort Canby sprang up around the lighthouse and is now a famous visitor's attraction.

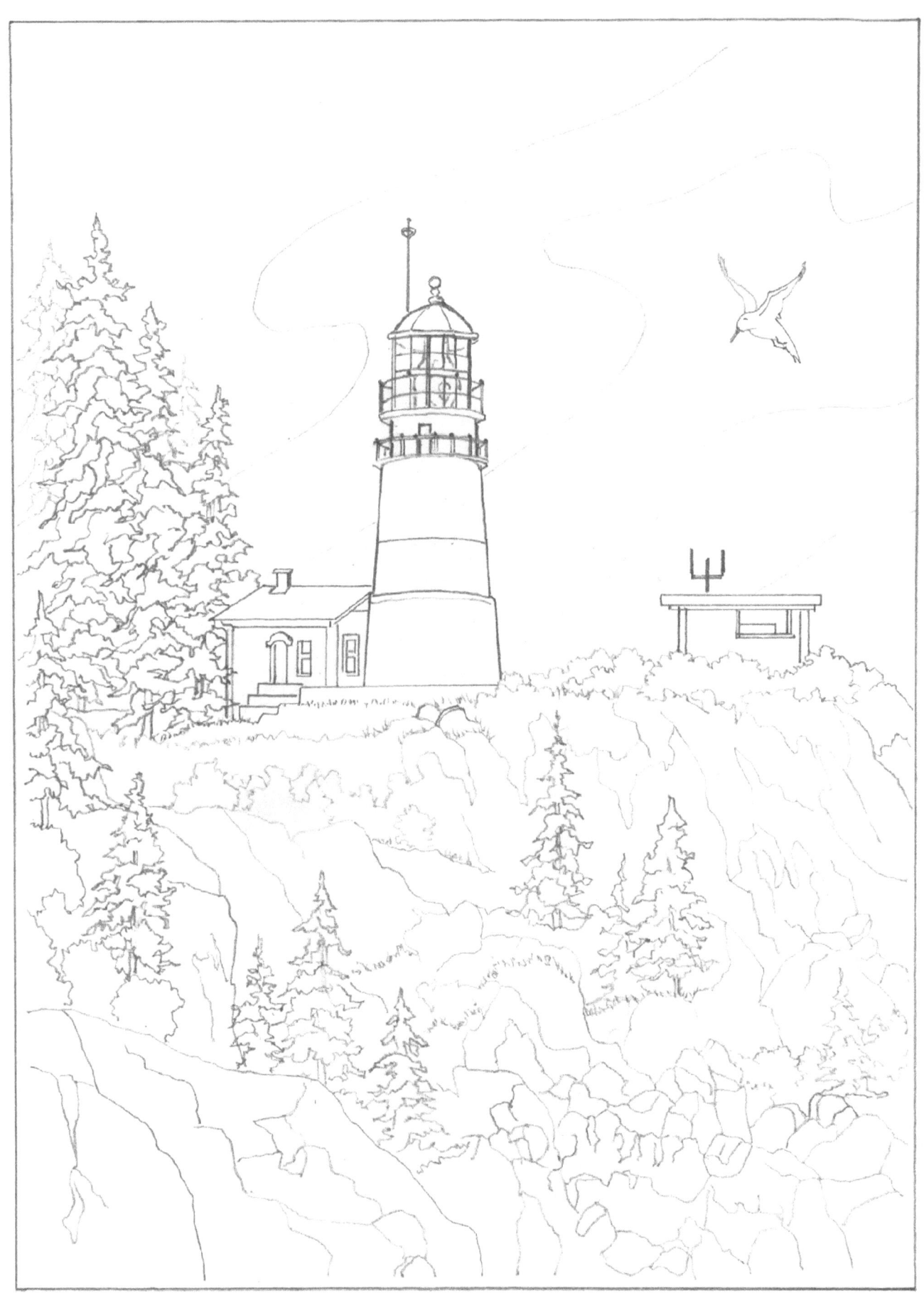

CAPE DISAPPOINTMENT - Ilwaco, WA

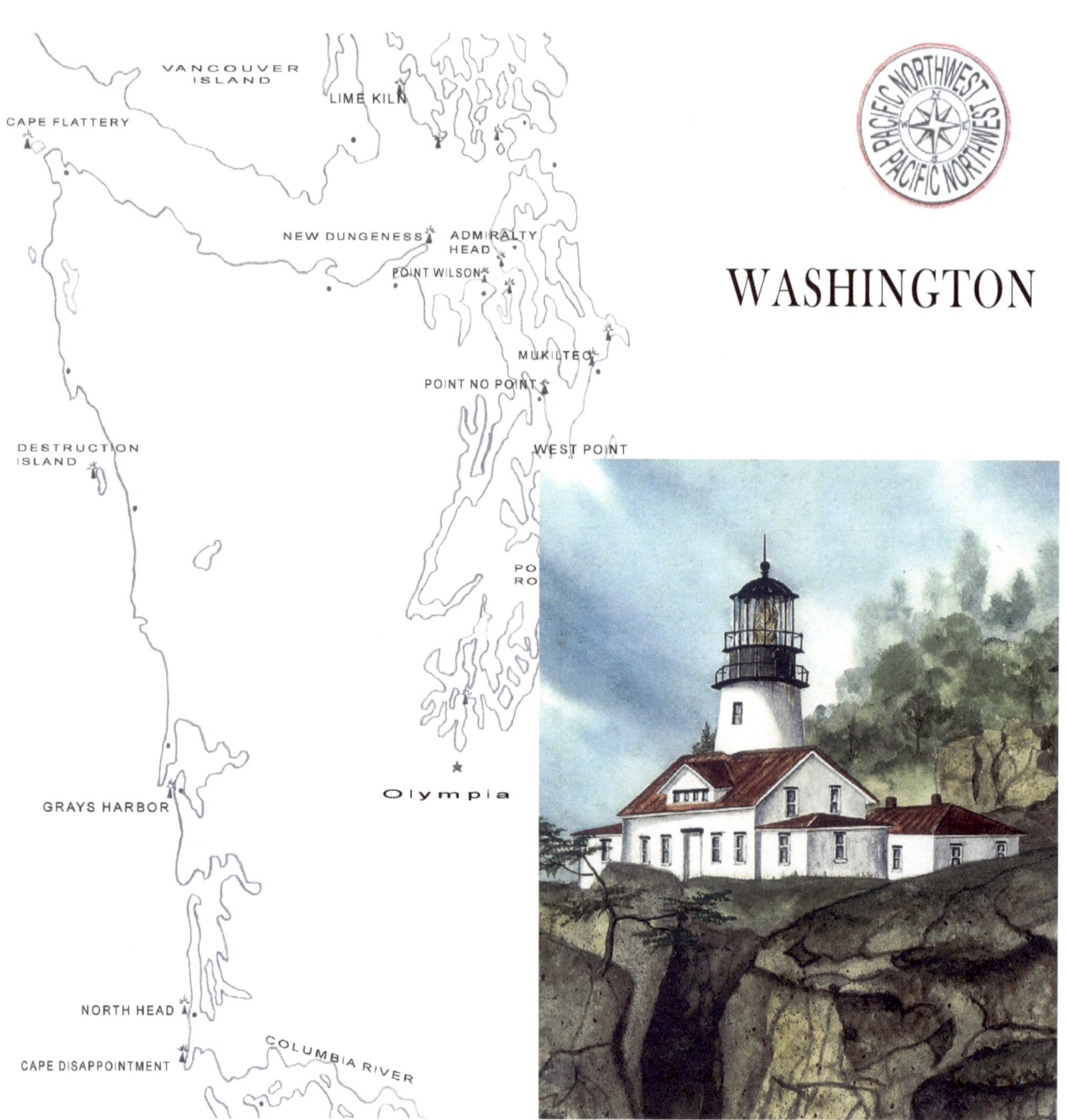

WASHINGTON

CAPE FLATTERY LIGHTHOUSE, located on Tatoosh Island, at the entrance to the Straight of Juan de Fuca, stands at the extreme northwesterly corner of the continental United States. Completed in 1857, the stone tower rises 165 feet above the sea and shines its' fourth-order lens out over the turbulant Pacific ocean. It's light still marks the cape. A U.S. Signal Corps weather station was established on the island in 1883. The lighthouse is now automated, and Coast Guard operators and maintenance personnel visit only occasionally.

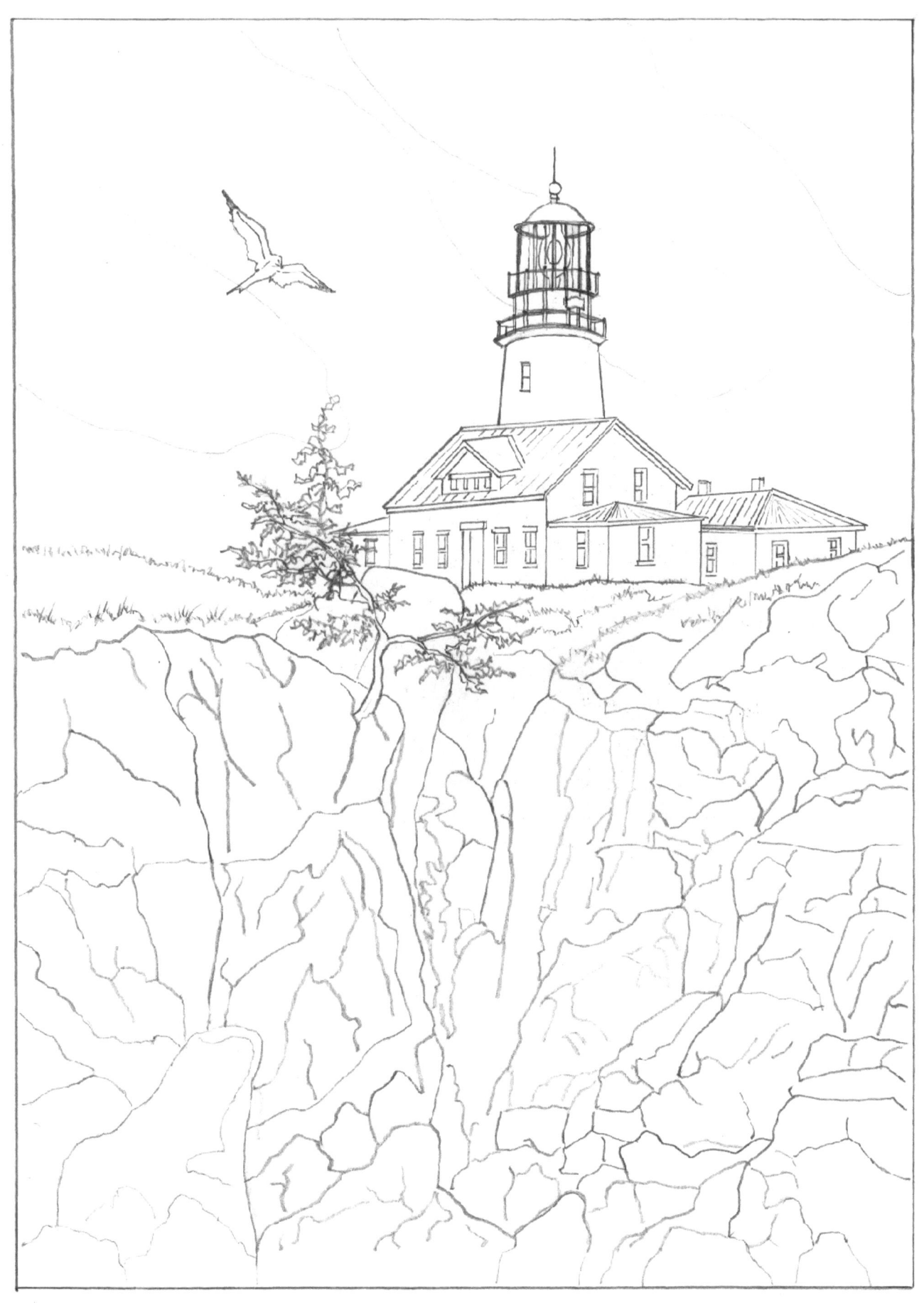

CAPE FLATTERY - Tatoosh Island, WA

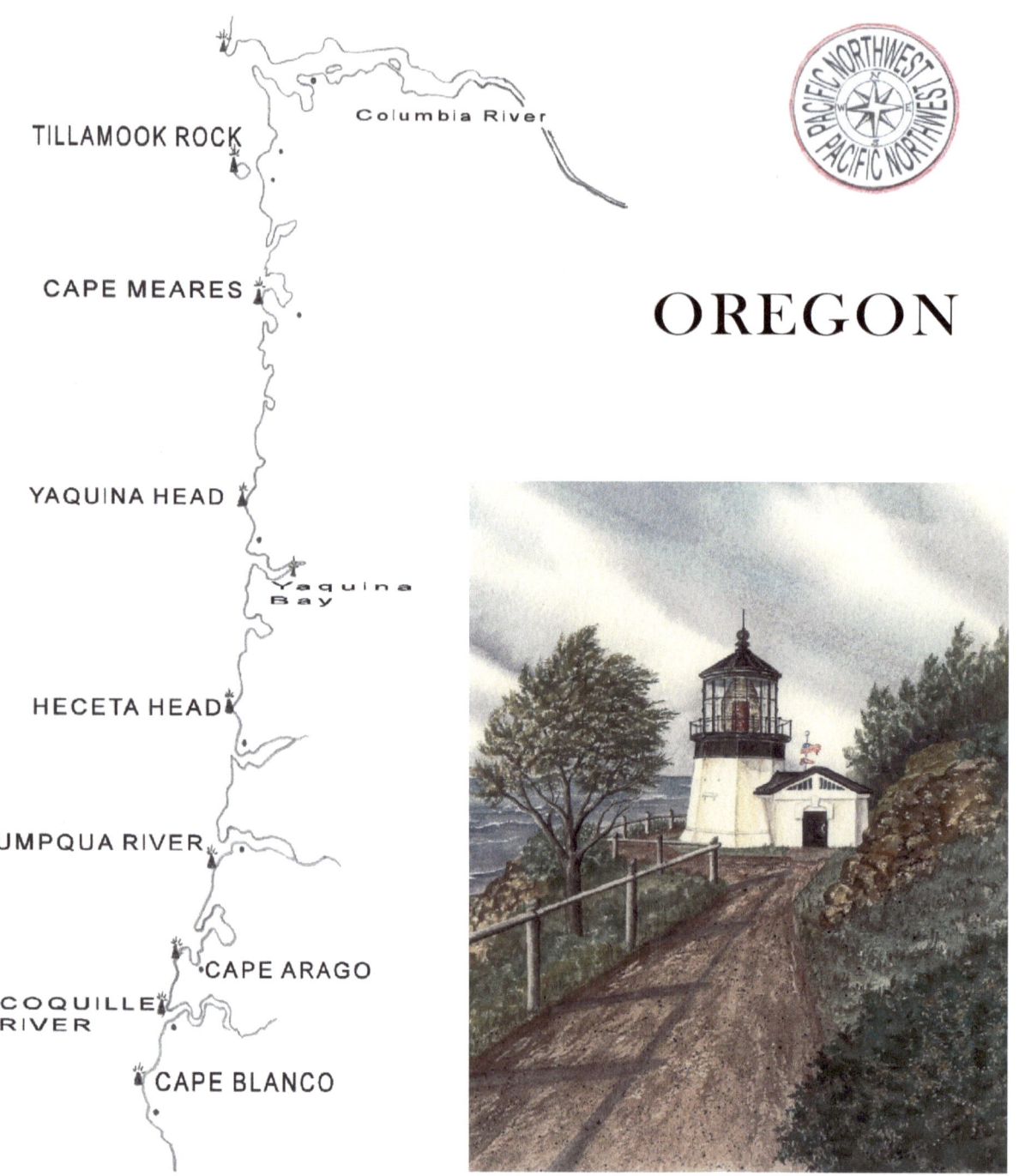

TILLAMOOK ROCK

Columbia River

CAPE MEARES

OREGON

YAQUINA HEAD

Yaquina Bay

HECETA HEAD

UMPQUA RIVER

CAPE ARAGO

COQUILLE RIVER

CAPE BLANCO

CAPE MEARES LIGHTHOUSE, established in 1890, is located several miles west of Tillamook. The thirty-eight foot octagonal, iron tower stands on a towering cliff 217 feet above the breakers. It was given a first-order Fresnel lens, illuminated by a coal-oil lamp, which made the light visible from twenty-one miles at sea. Nearby is Cape Meares National Refuge.

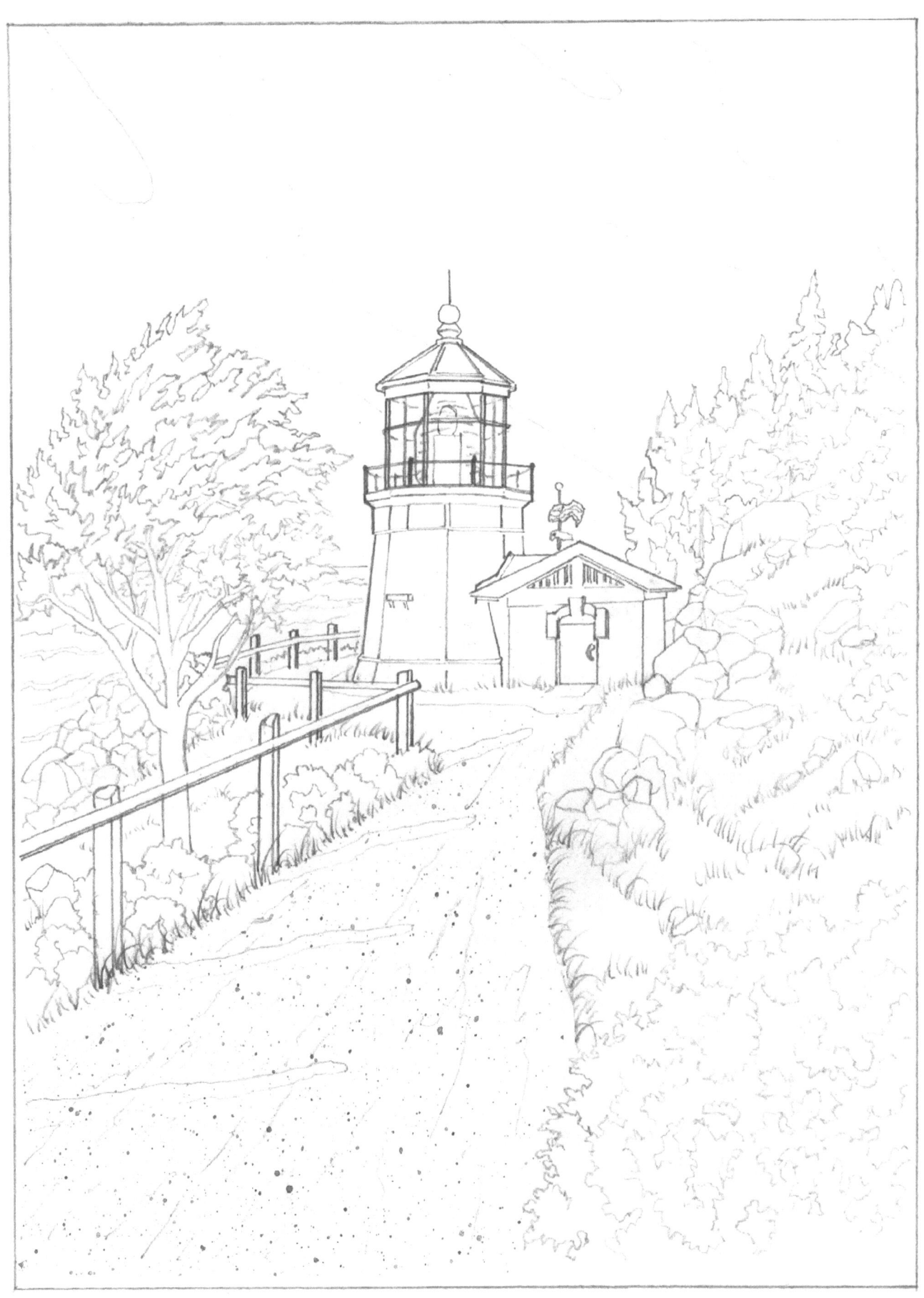

CAPE MEARES - Tillamook, OR

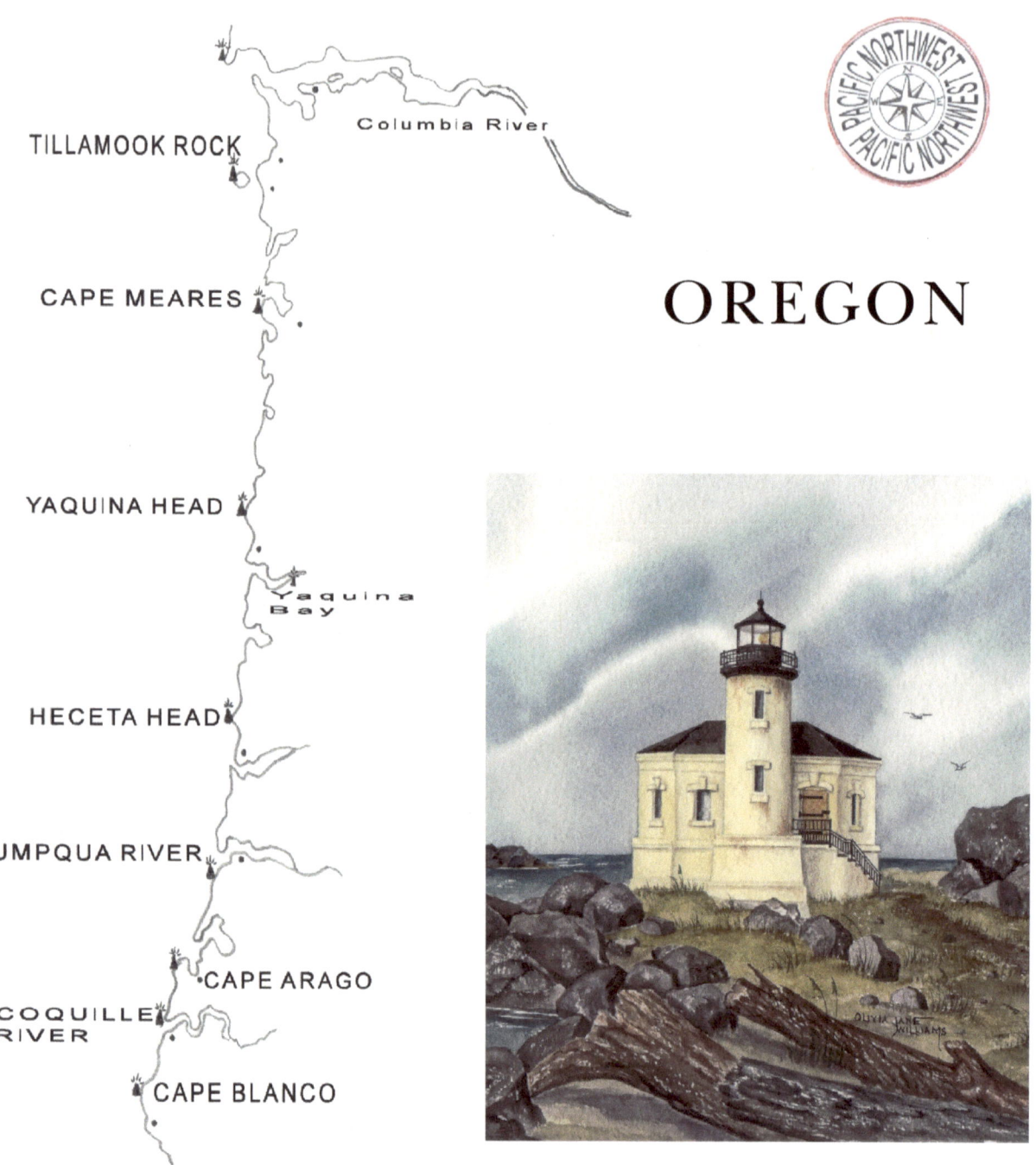

OREGON

TILLAMOOK ROCK

CAPE MEARES

YAQUINA HEAD

Yaquina Bay

HECETA HEAD

UMPQUA RIVER

CAPE ARAGO

COQUILLE RIVER

CAPE BLANCO

Columbia River

COQUILLE RIVER LIGHTHOUSE, near Bandon, was given a fourth order Fresnel lens and completed in 1895 at a cost of $17,600. It's unique forty foot masonry tower sits next to Coquille Bar, considered one of the most dangerous on the West Coast. It served both as a harbor entrance light and seacoast beacon.

The Coast Guard abandoned the light in 1939, and it sat deteriorating for several years. Restored in recent years, it is now an historic attraction of Bullards Beach State Park.

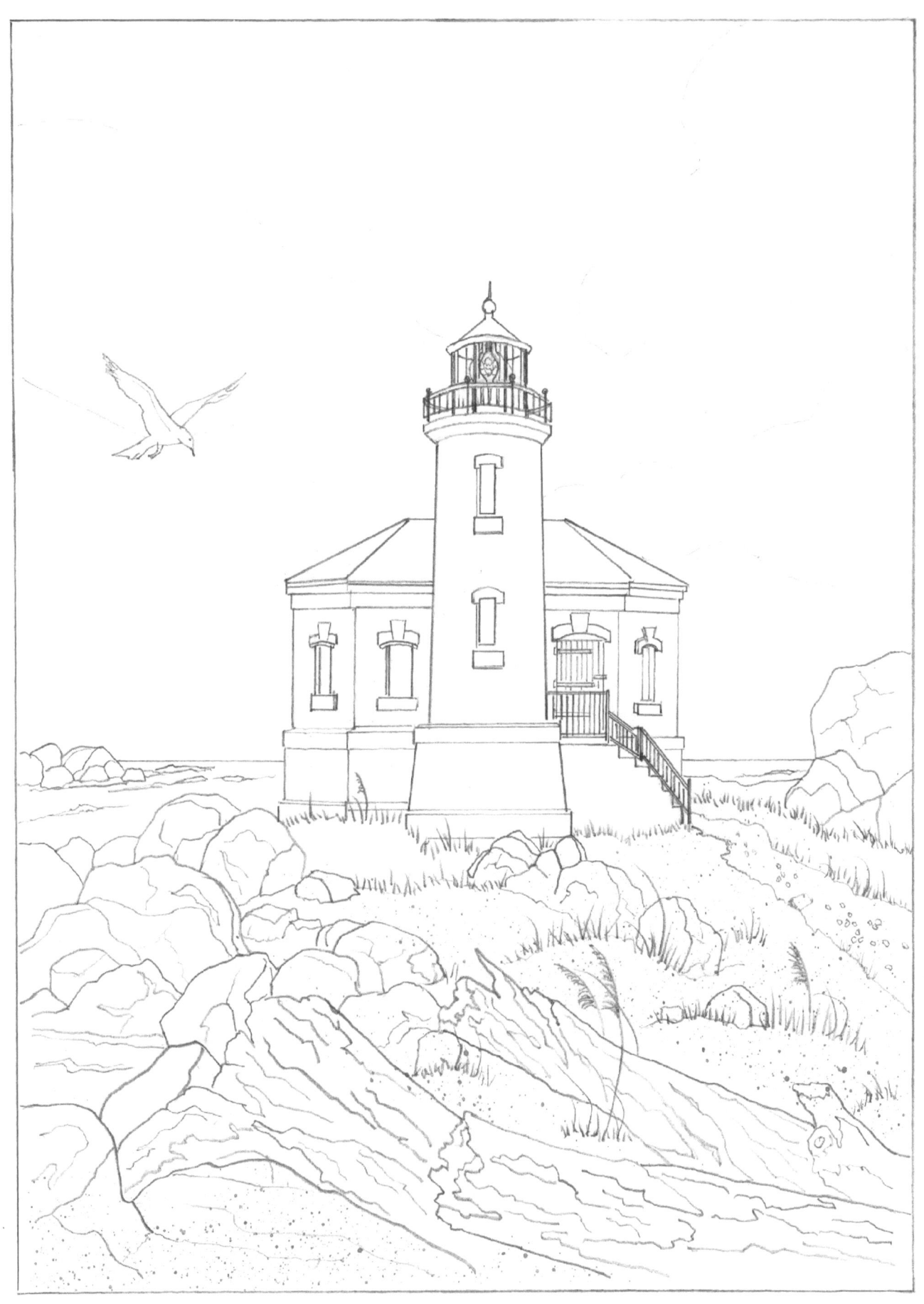

COQUILLE RIVER - Bandon, OR

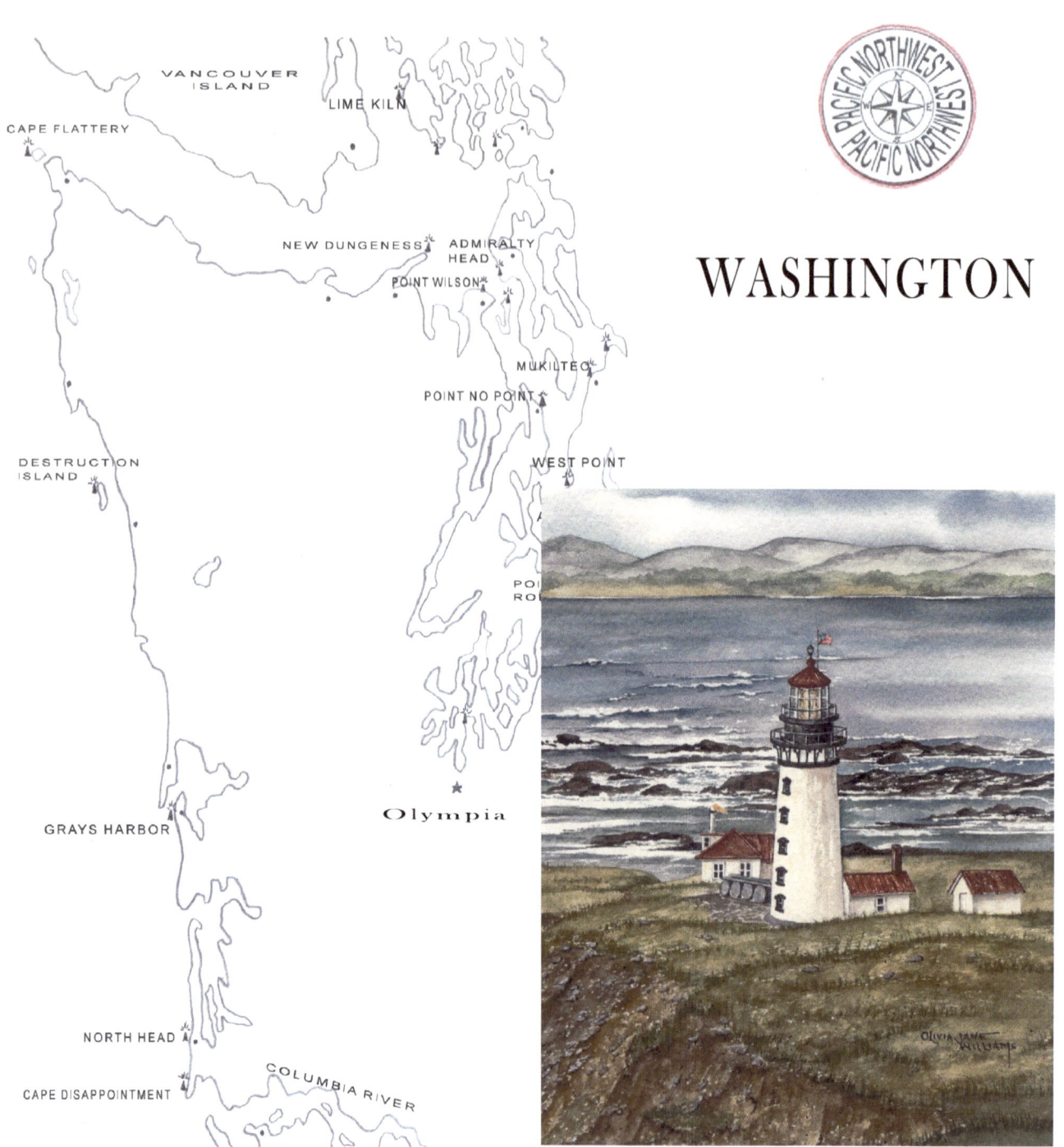

WASHINGTON

DESTRUCTION ISLAND LIGHTHOUSE, located on an island three miles off the Olympic Peninsula of Western Washington, was activated New Year's Eve 1891. The masonry tower has a 115 step staircase and is ninety-four feet high and encased in iron. The lantern housed a first-order Fresnel lens with 1,176 glass prisims, including twenty-four bulls-eyes. The lighthouse can be seen from Highway 101 about a mile south of Ruby Beach near La Push.

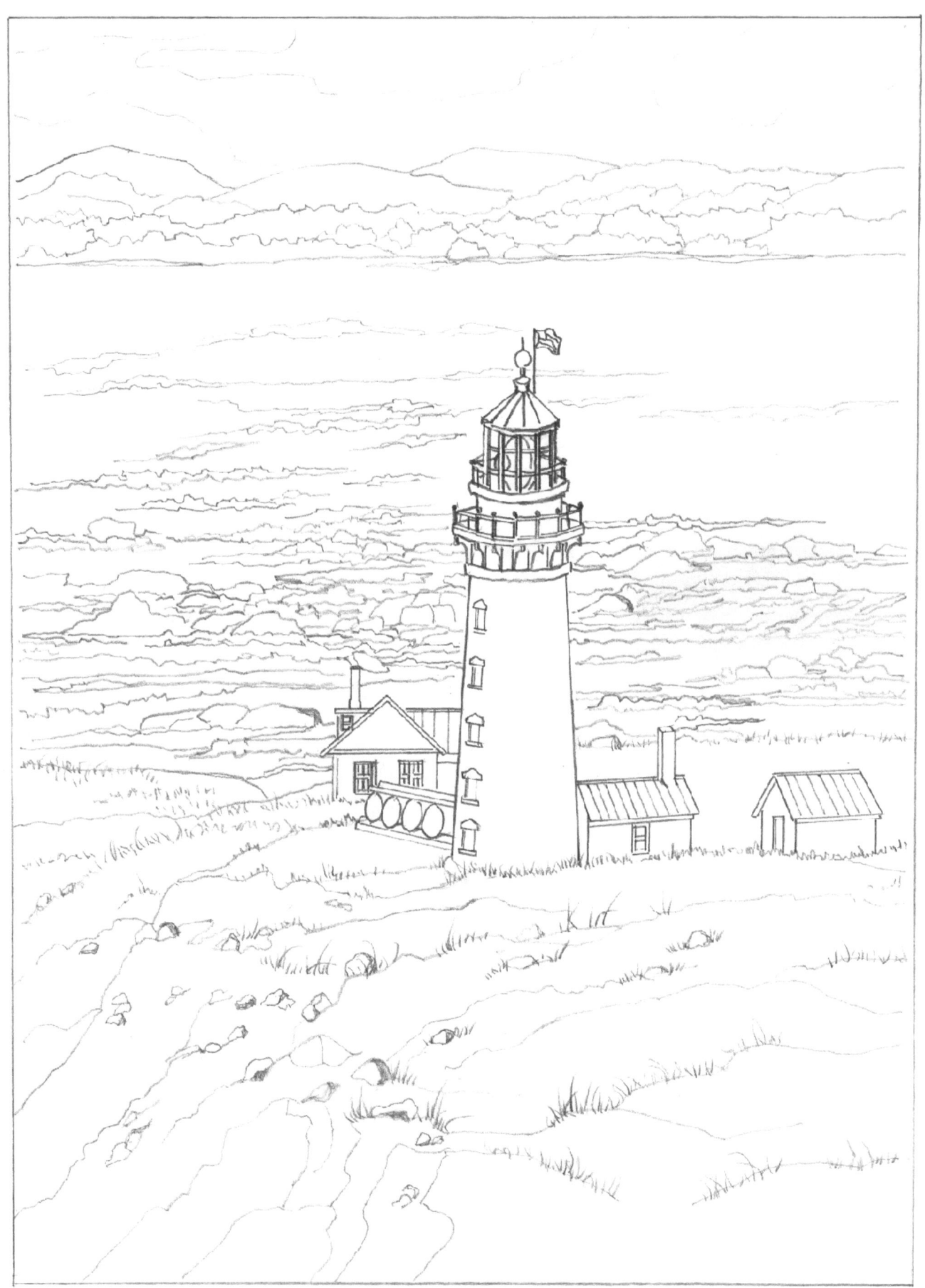

DESTRUCTION ISLAND - La Push, WA

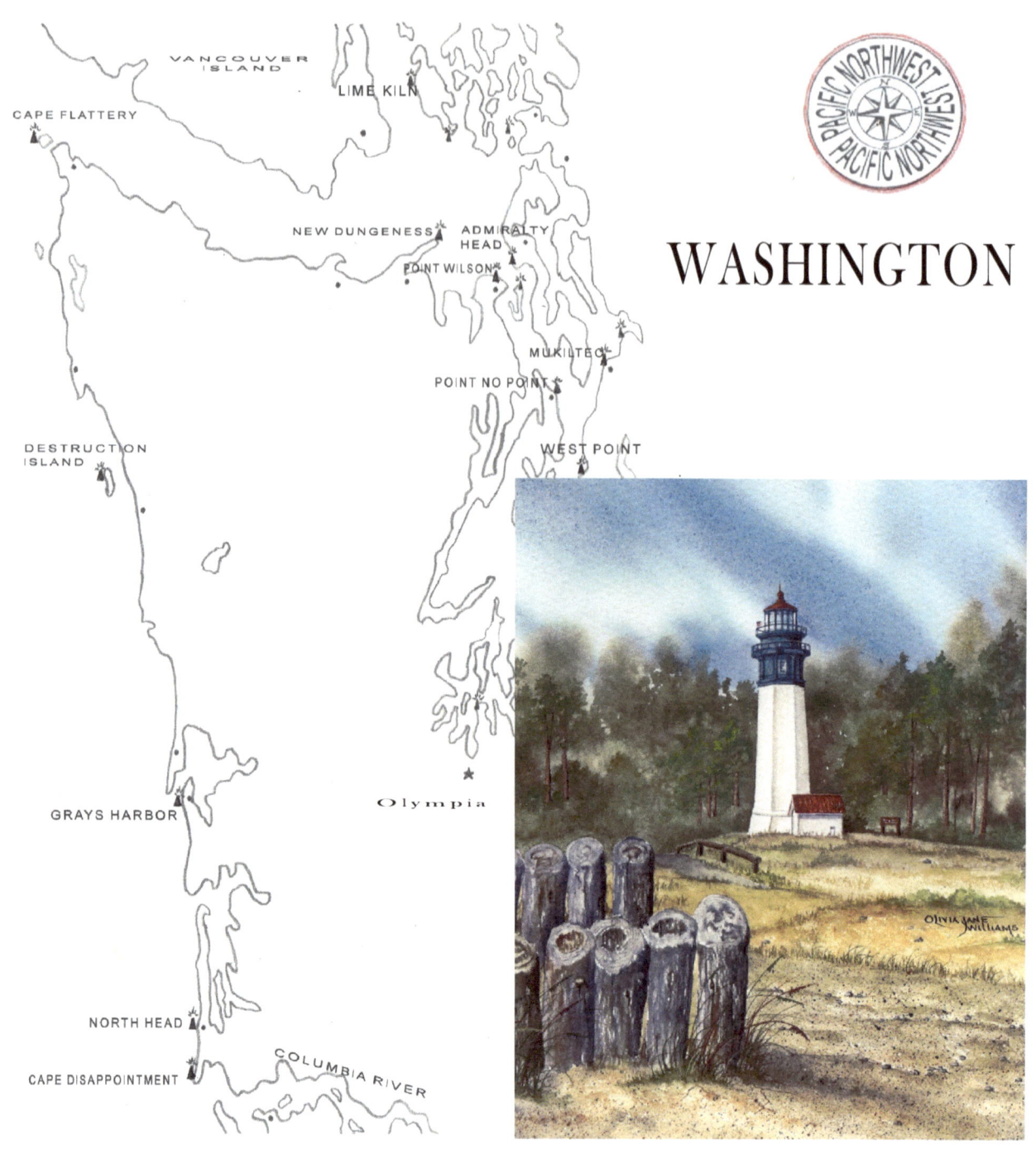

WASHINGTON

GRAYS HARBOR LIGHTHOUSE, located near Westport, was completed in 1898, and is one of the tallest on the West Coast. It's octagonal masonry tower stands more than a 100 feet from base to lantern, and houses a third-order Fresnel lens. Near the lighthouse, a fog signal and radio beacon are maintained to aid commercial fishing vessels and deep-sea cargo ships entering and departing.

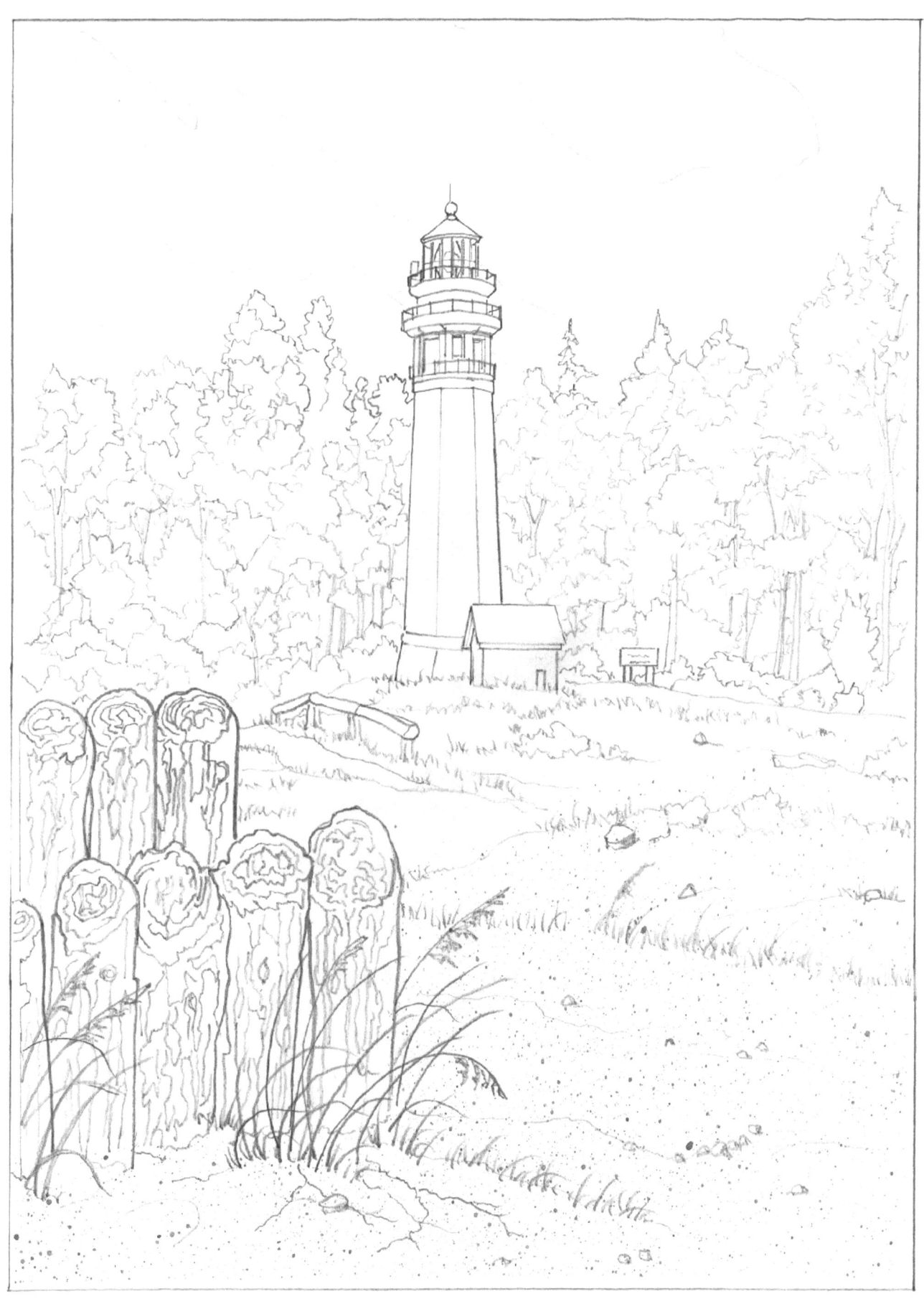

GRAYS HARBOR - Westport, WA

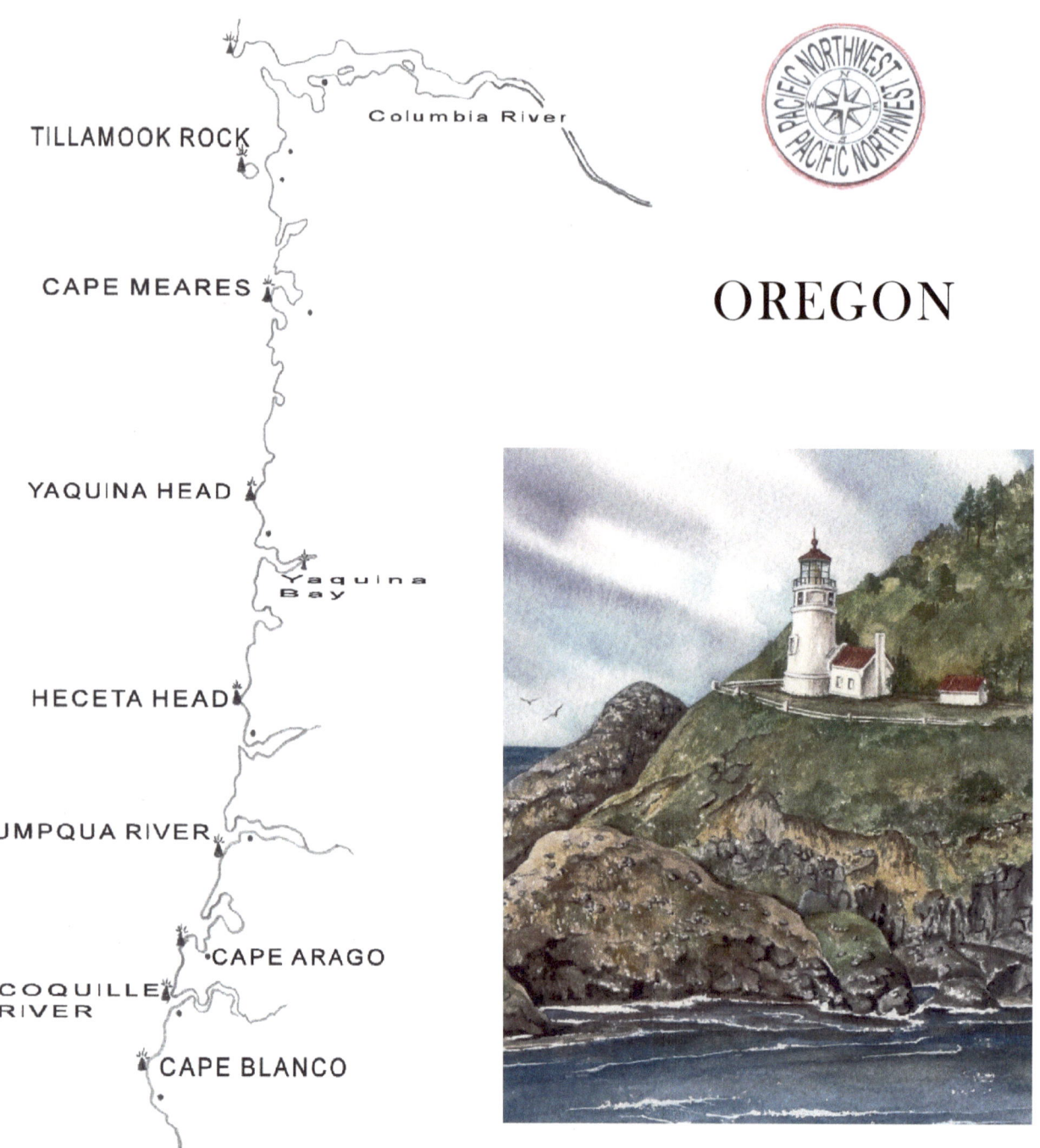

TILLAMOOK ROCK

Columbia River

CAPE MEARES

OREGON

YAQUINA HEAD

Yaquina Bay

HECETA HEAD

UMPQUA RIVER

CAPE ARAGO

COQUILLE RIVER

CAPE BLANCO

HECETA HEAD LIGHTHOUSE, north of Florence, was completed in 1894. The sixty-five foot masonry structure overlooks the headland that marks its' name. In 1775, Captian Don Bruno de Heceta, of the Spanish Royal Navy, led an expedition along the coast of the Pacific Northwest. Heceta waters charted craggy rock reaching far out into the ocean; dangerous to sea vessels. Equipped with a large first-order Fresnel lens, and the height of its' perch on the cliffs, the beam can be seen from twenty-one miles at sea.

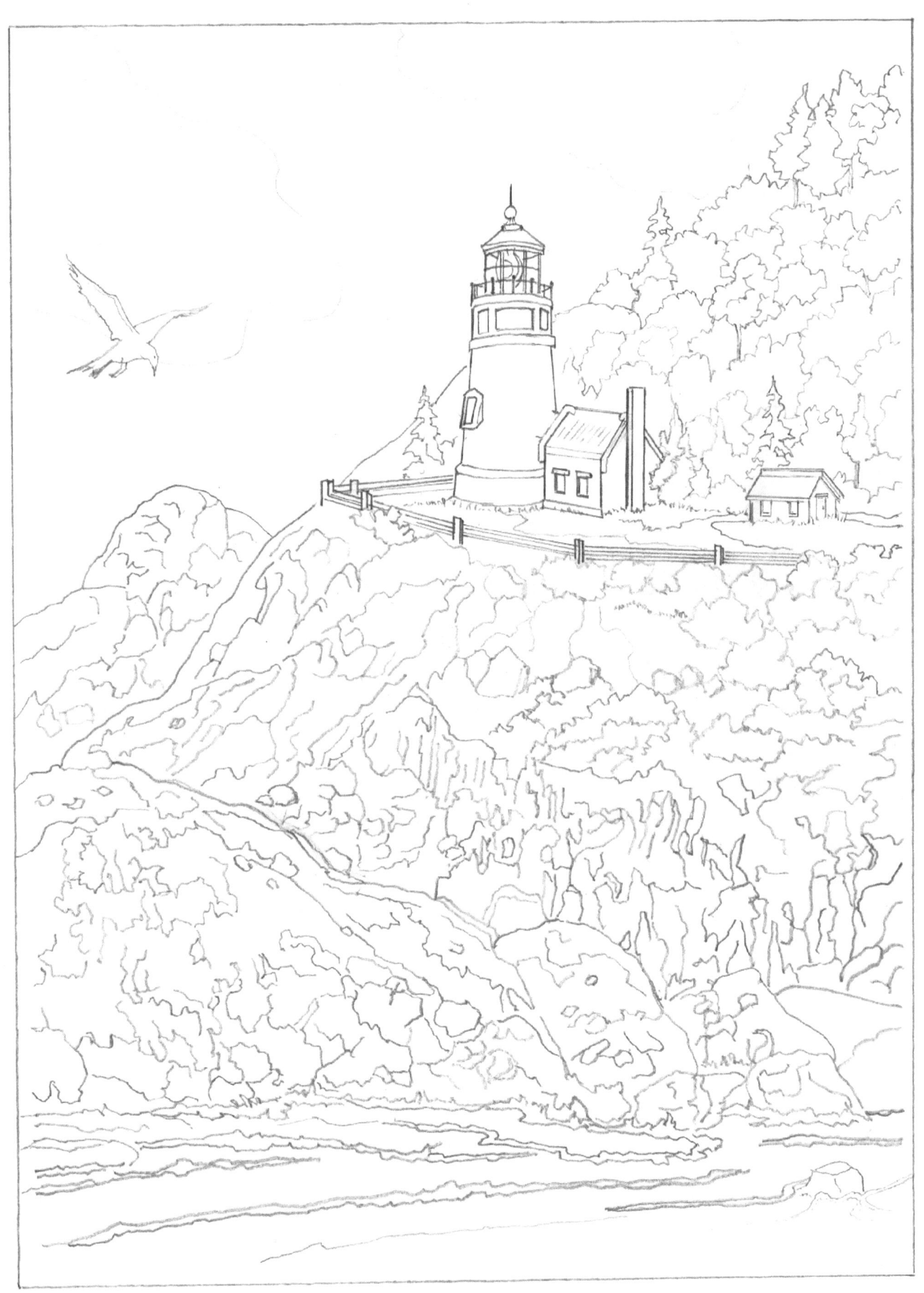

HECETA HEAD - Florence, OR

WASHINGTON

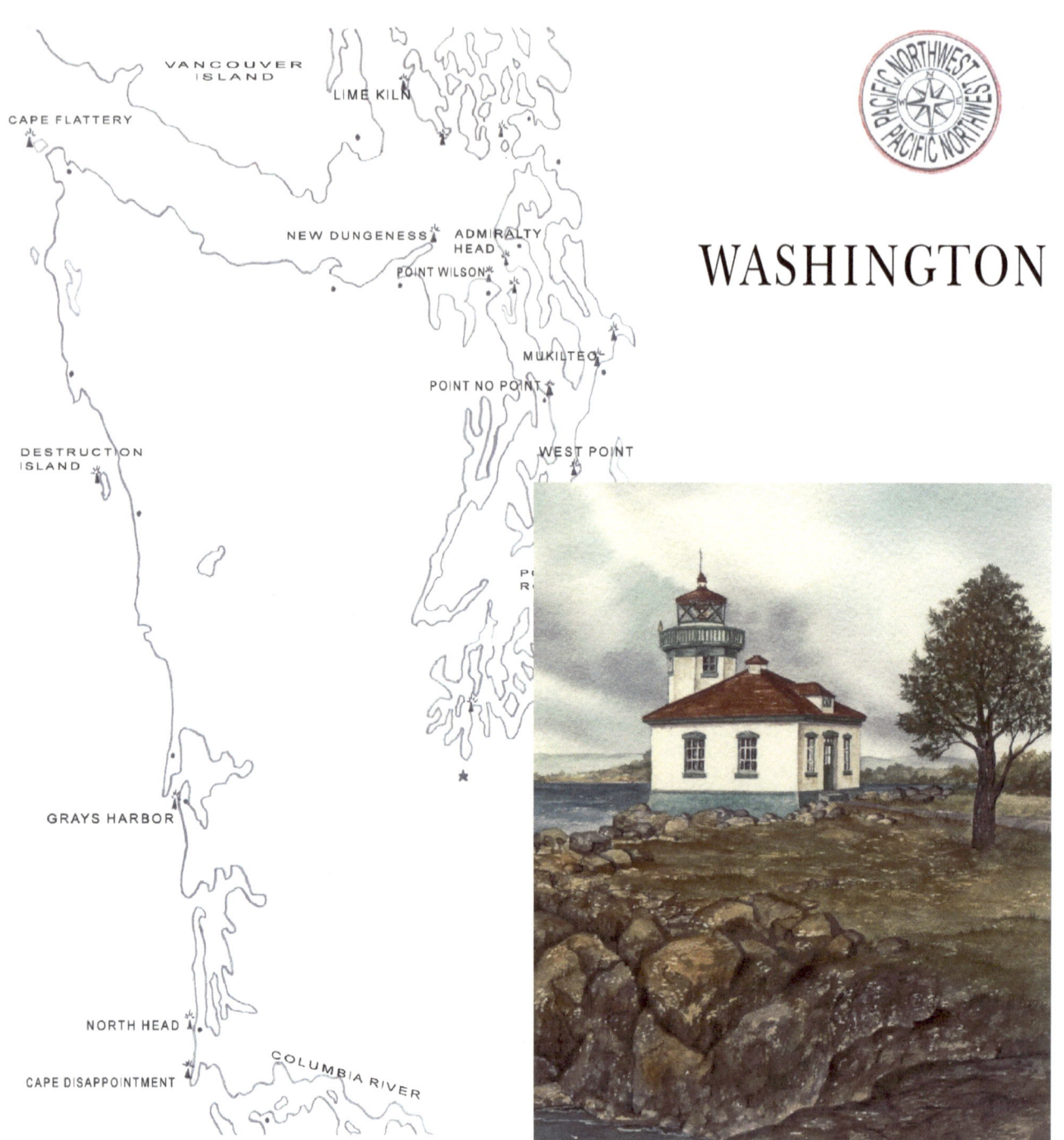

LIME KILN LIGHTHOUSE, built on San Juan Island in 1914, features a thirty-eight foot octagonal tower attached to a fog signal building. The lighthouse gets it's name from the lime rock cliffs and once productive lime kilns. It was the last major lighthouse in the state to receive electricity. Oil vapor lamps in prismatic lens provided the light source until WWII due to the cost of extending an underwater cable from the mainland. Lime Kiln is now a favorite site for whale watching.

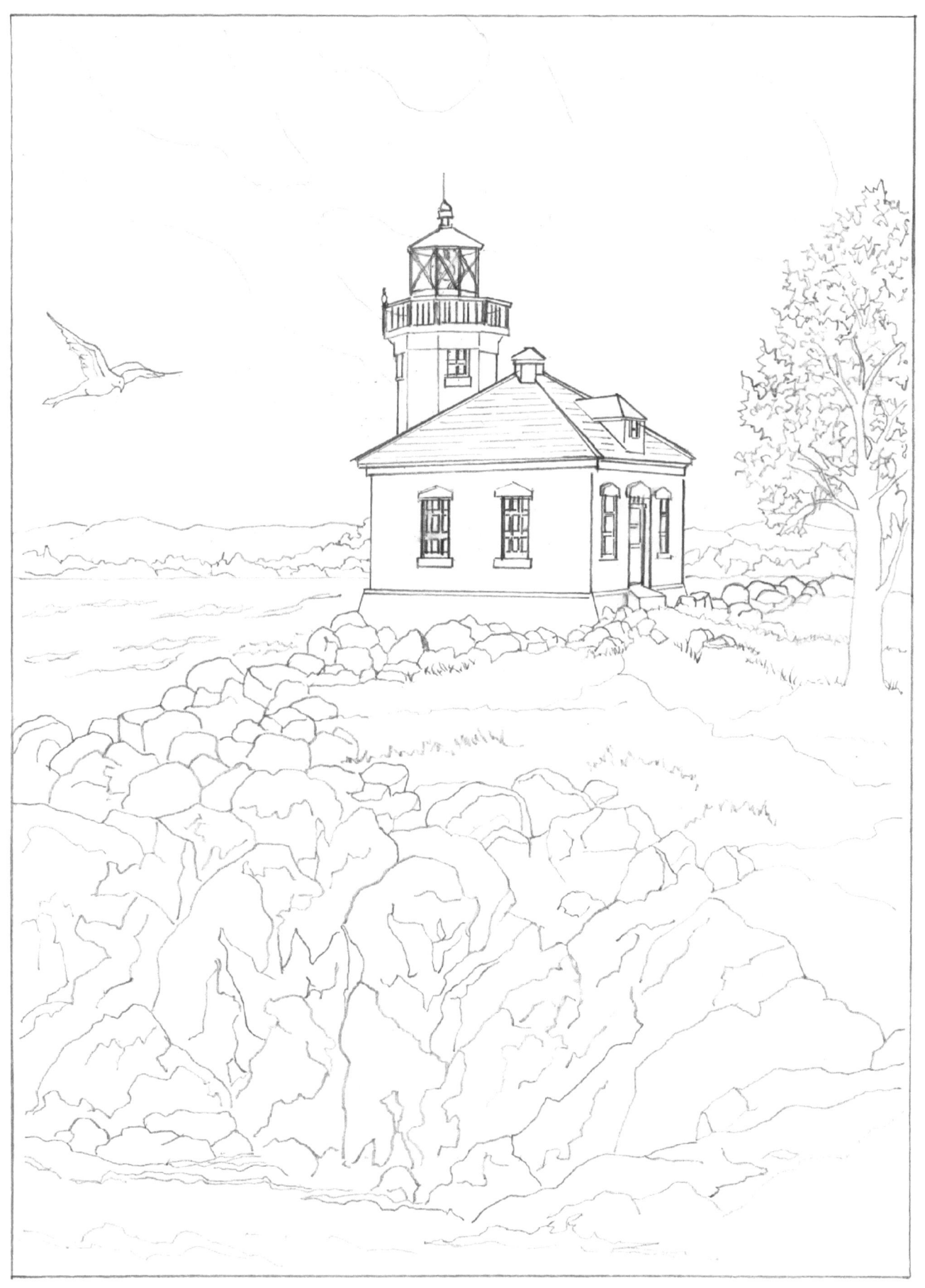

LIME KILN - San Juan Island, WA

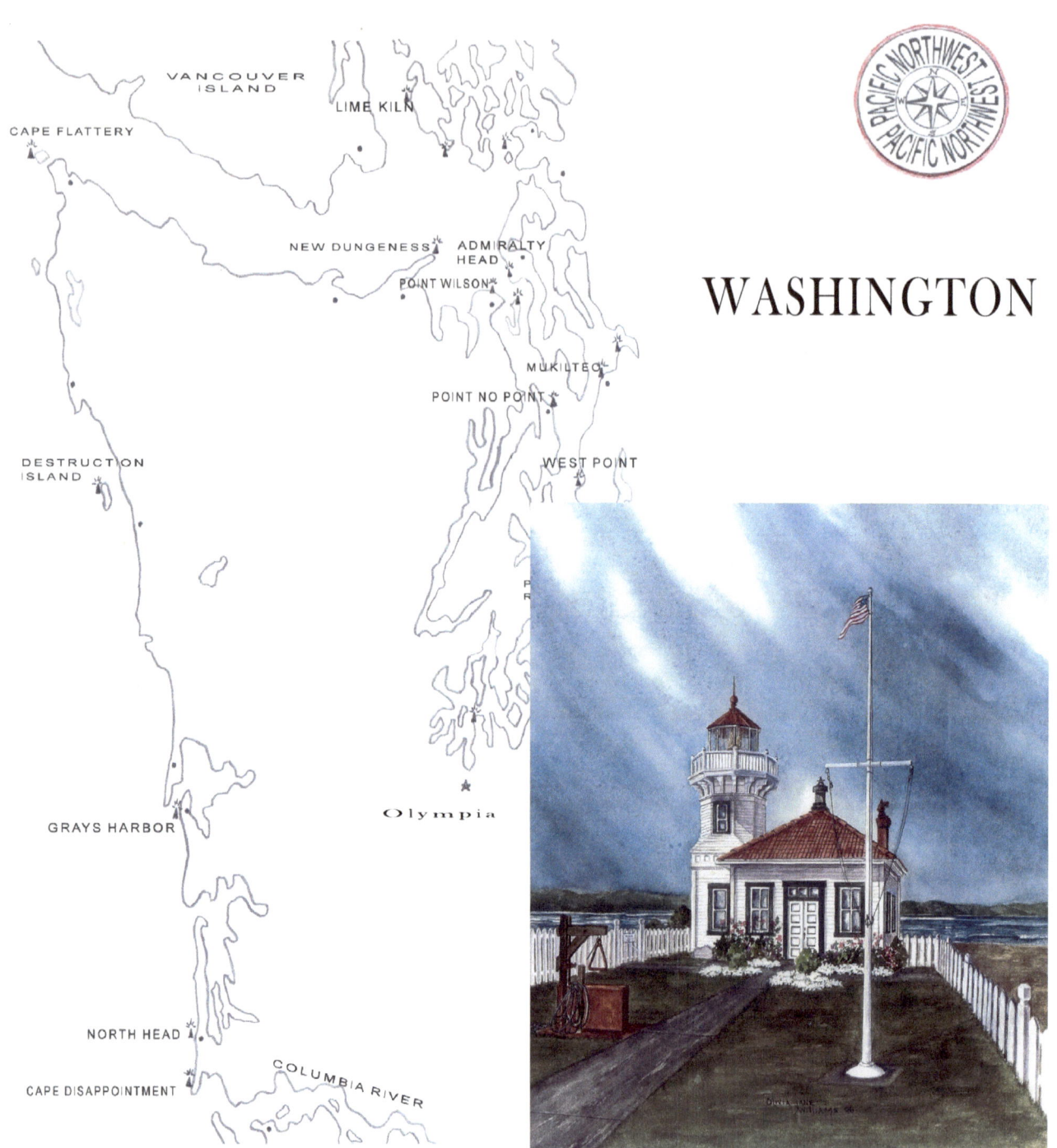

WASHINGTON

MUKILTEO LIGHTHOUSE active since 1906, is located in Mukilteo near the Whidbey Island ferry landing. The thirty-foot, octagonal, wood frame, Victorian style structure, houses a fourth-order Fresnel lens and a Daboll trumpet to warn ships during heavy fog. On Elliot Point, where the lighthouse stands, a treaty signed by Gov. Isaac Stevens and the Northwestern Indian Chiefs ceded all lands from Pully Point northward to the whites.

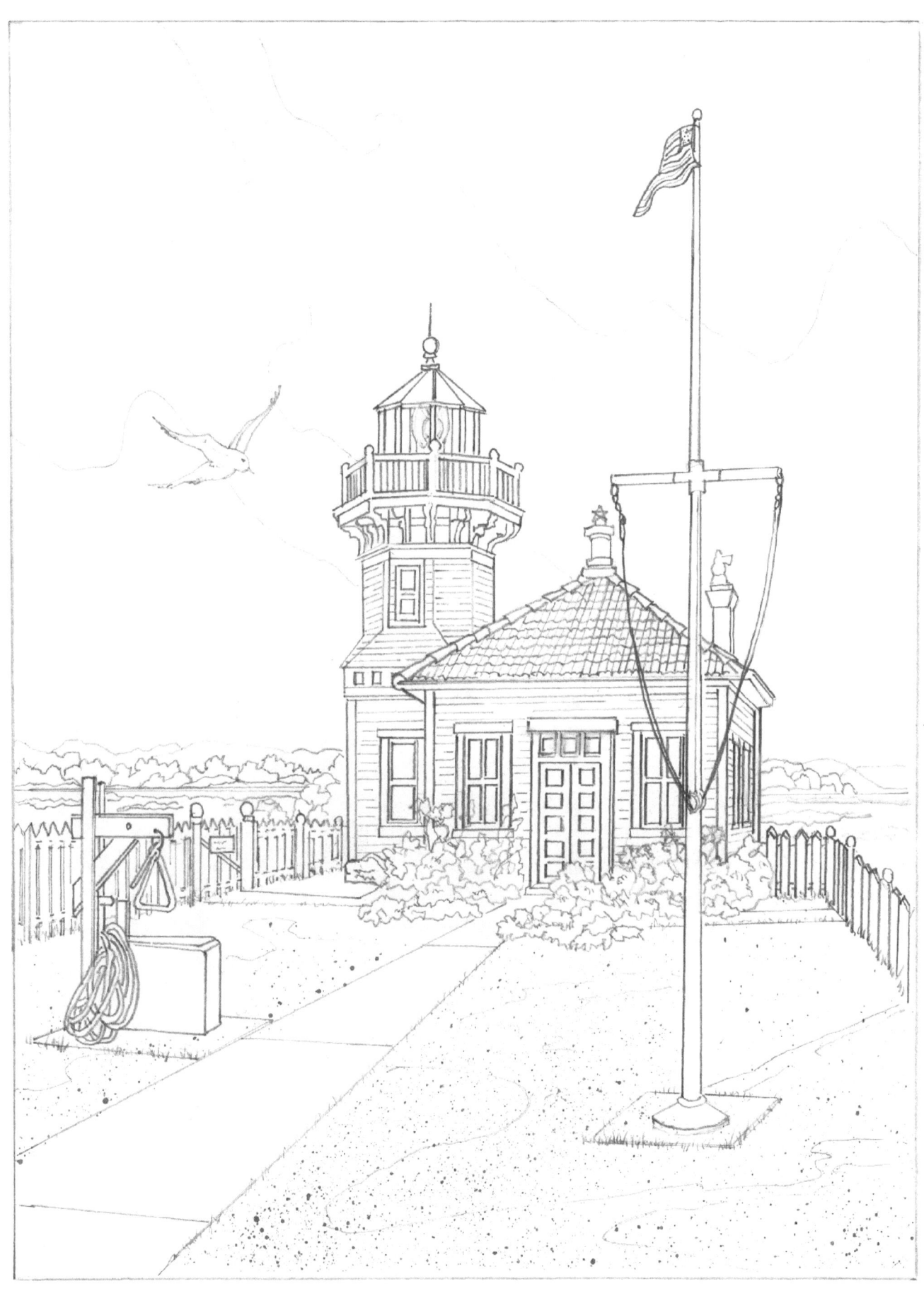

MUKILTEO - Mukilteo, WA

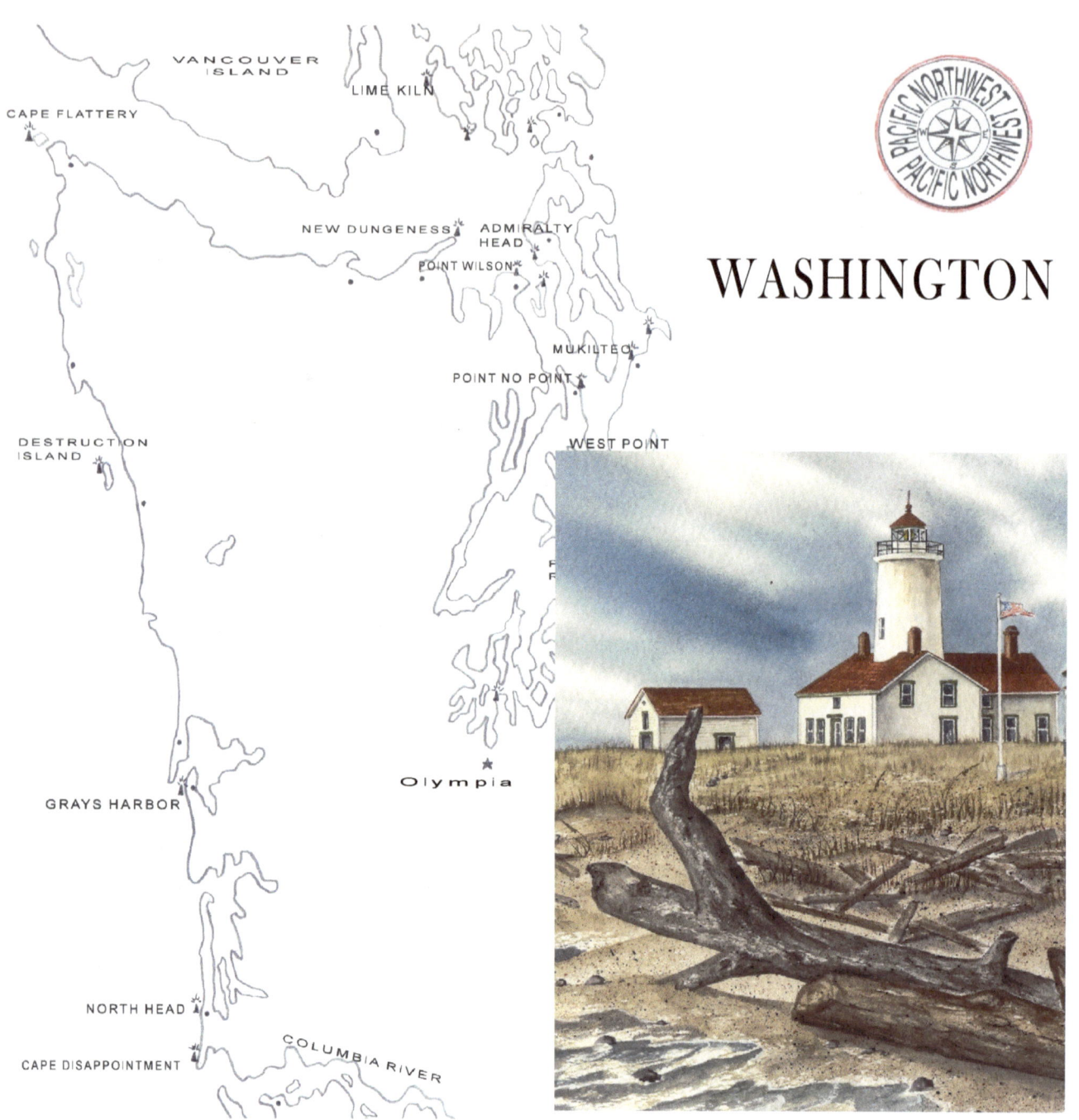

WASHINGTON

NEW DUNGENESS LIGHTHOUSE, located at the end of an eight-mile spit from Sequim, jutting into the Straight of Juan de Fuca, was constructed in 1857. The eighty-nine foot tower was equipped with a third-order Fresnel lens. In 1927, due to the deterioration of the upper part of the structure, it was reduced to a height of sixty-three feet, and the old lantern was replaced by the abandoned tower at Admiralty Head. In the nineteenth century, the sandspit near the lighthouse was a battleground for invading Indian tribes.

With the increasing numbers of cargo vessels entering the strait, the station's light, fog signal and radio beacon are a critical aid to navigation.

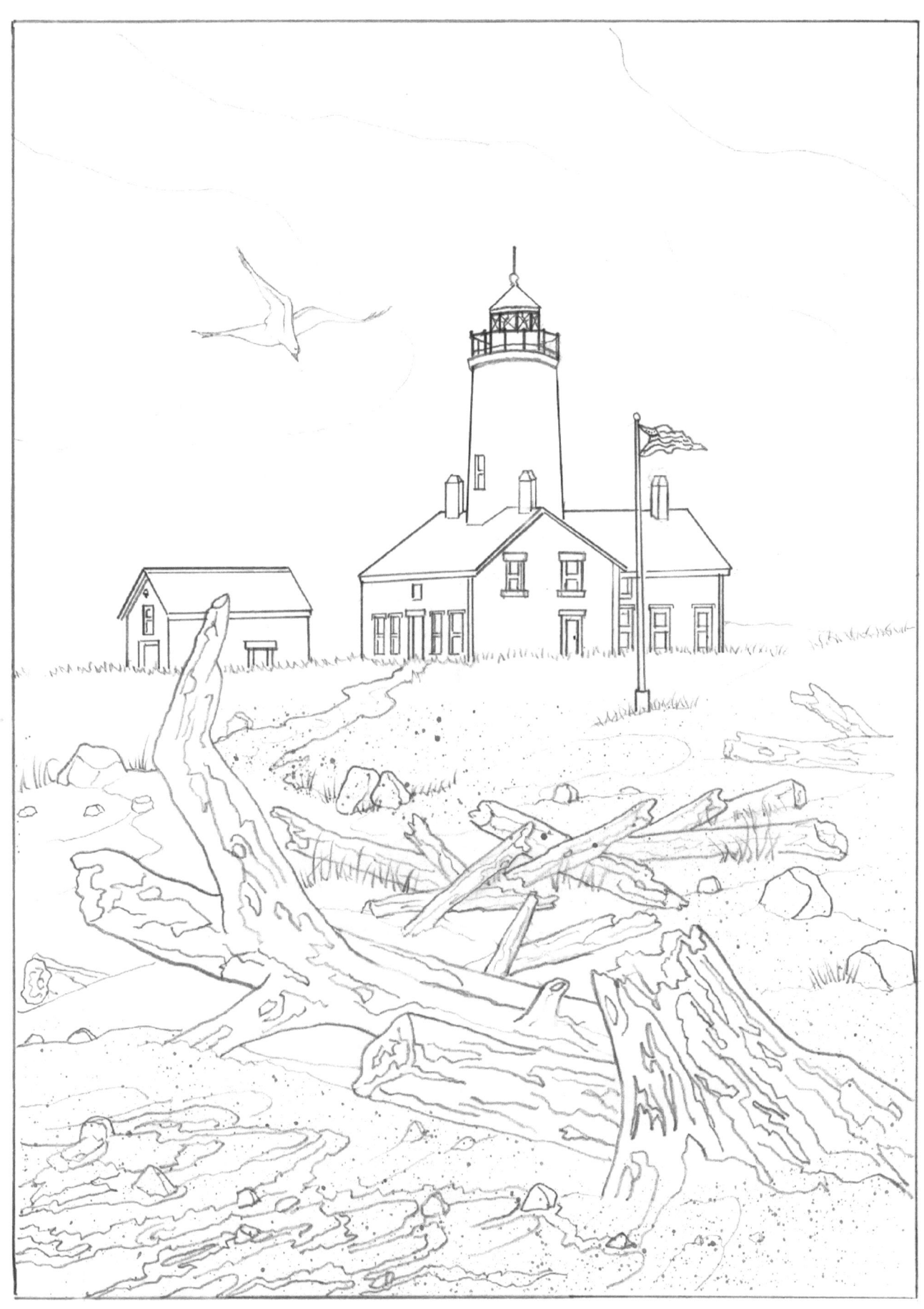

NEW DUNGENESS - Sequim, WA

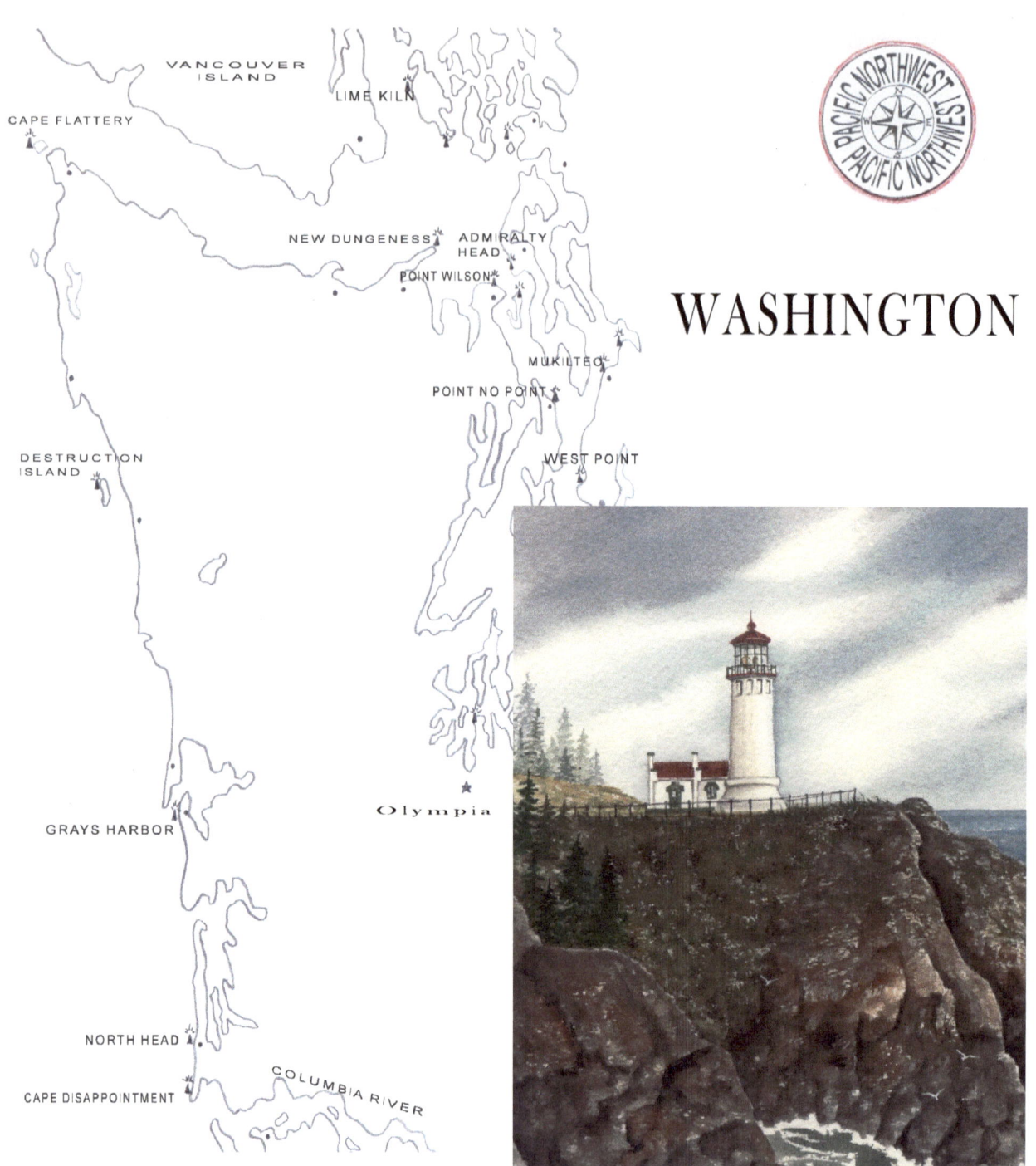

WASHINGTON

NORTH HEAD LIGHTHOUSE, near Ilwaco, completed in 1898, was built to warn ships approaching the Columbia River from the north. The sixty-five foot masonry tower stands on the edge of a cliff almost 130 feet high making the light from its fourth-order lens visible to ocean vessels at a great distance. The light was automated in 1961.

The station's two dwellings are now occupied by Fort Canby State Park personnel. The original lens can be seen at the Lewis and Clark Interpretive Center at Fort Canby.

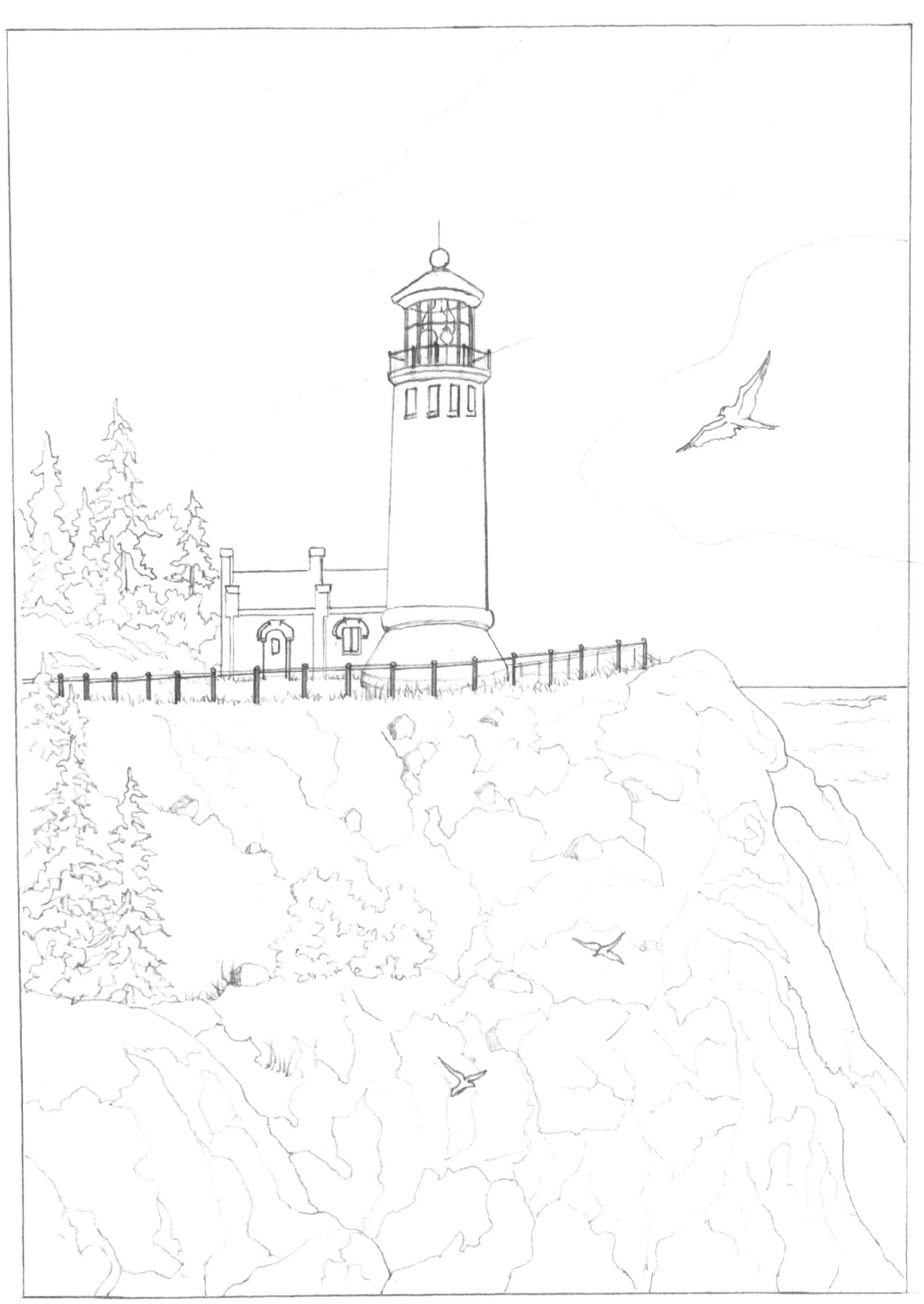

NORTH HEAD - Ilwaco, WA

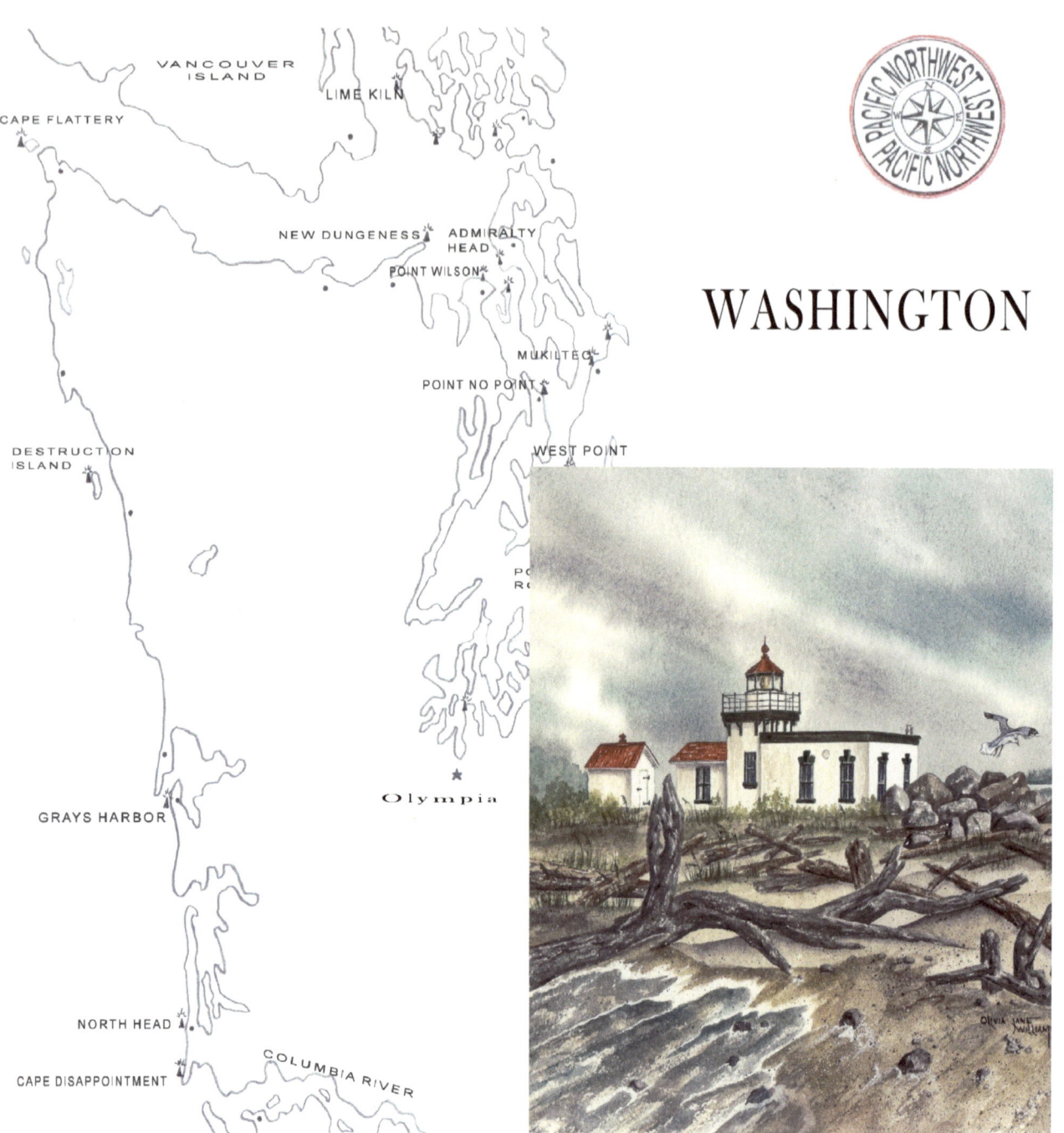

WASHINGTON

POINT NO POINT, first lighted in January, 1880 showed a fixed white light around 270 degrees of the horizon. A bell tower with fog bell was installed nearby, and later a fog signal building was attached to the tower. Located near Hansville on the Kitsap Peninsular, it became an historic site where one thousand members of the Chimacum, Skokomish and Clallam indian tribes signed a treaty with Gov. Issac Stevens which ended the territory's indian wars.

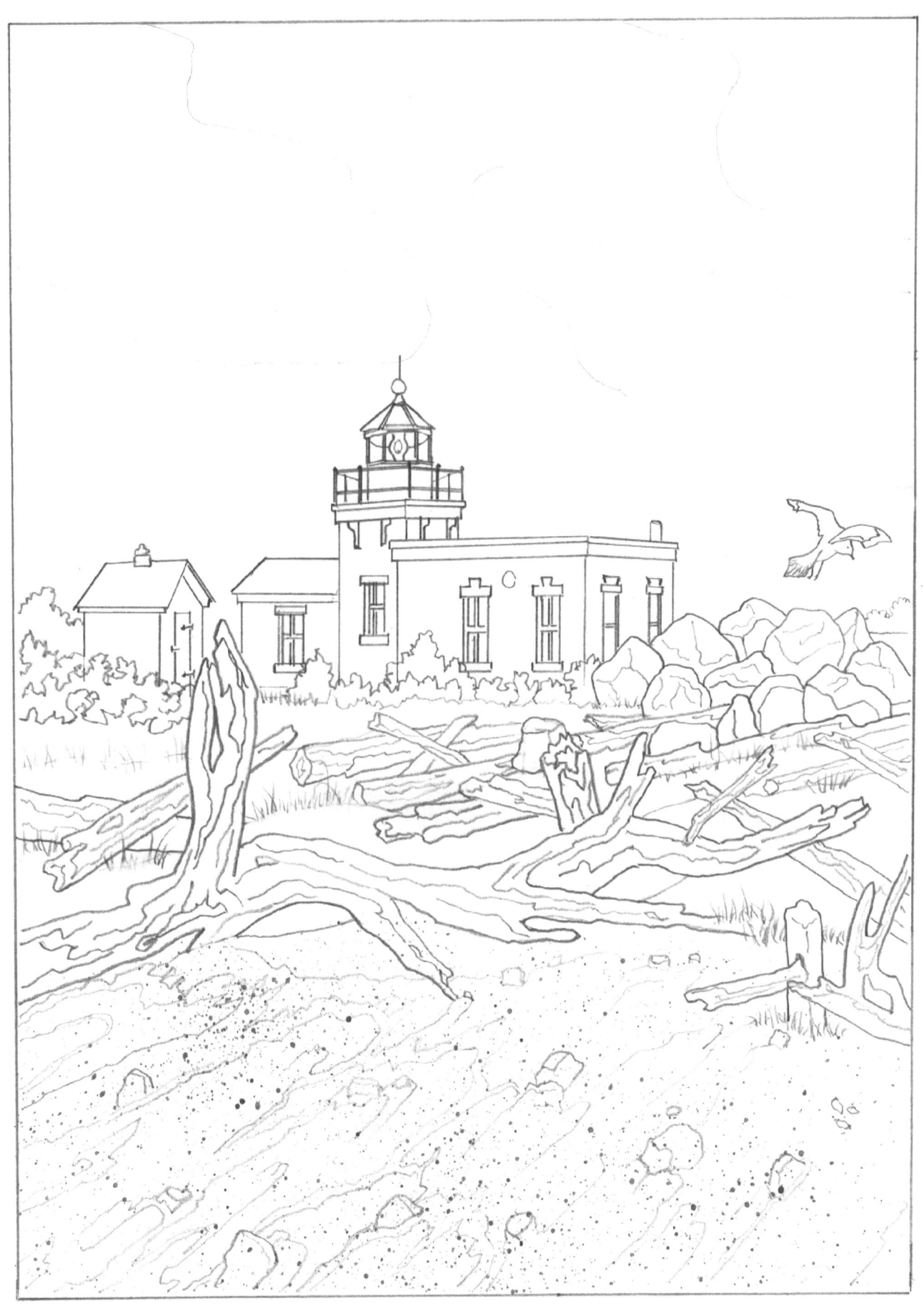

POINT NO POINT - Hansville, WA

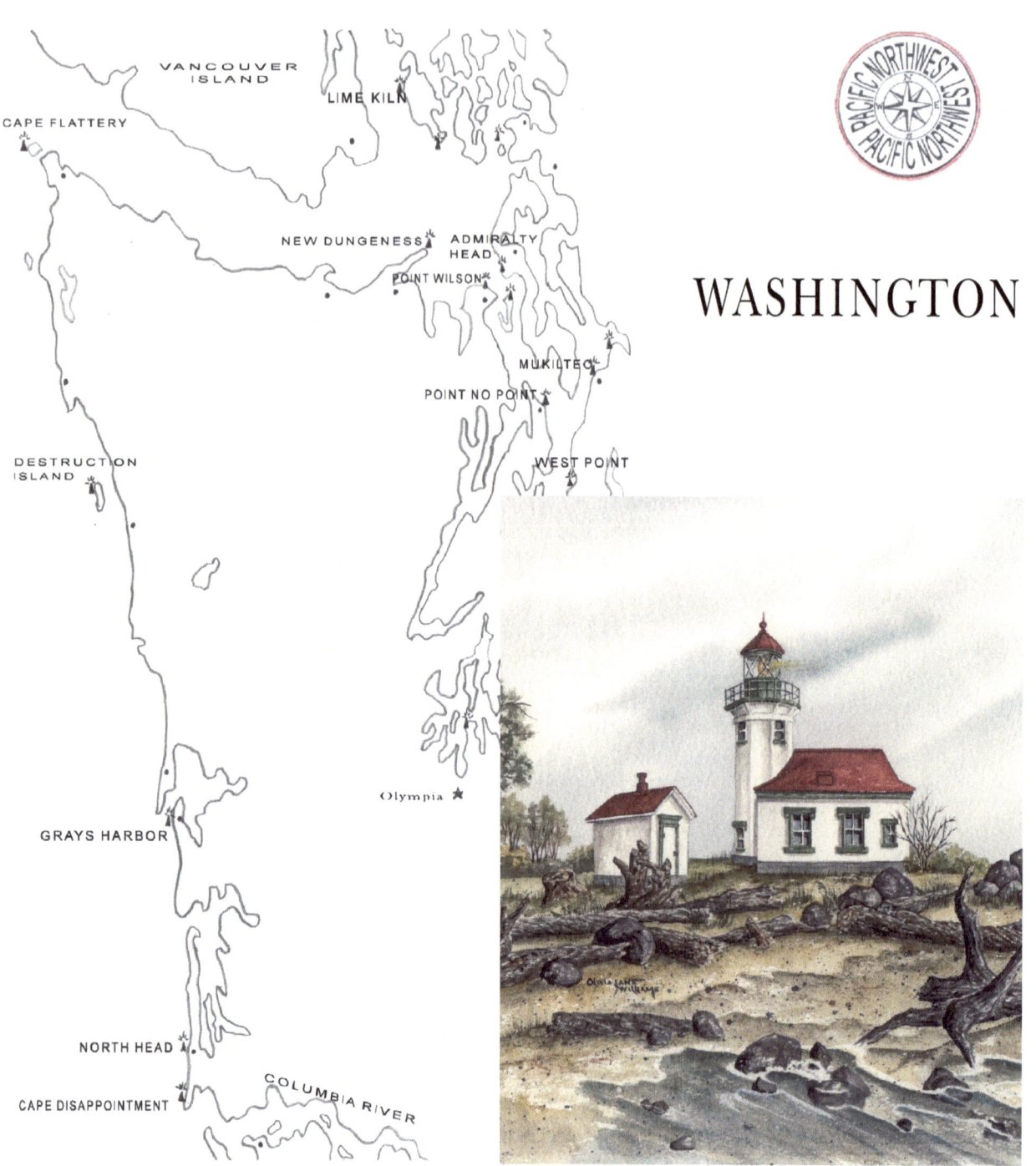

WASHINGTON

POINT ROBINSON LIGHTHOUSE located at the eastern end of Maury Island, was established as a fog signal station in July, 1885. The current structure, a thirty-eight foot octagonal tower, built in 1915, is situated at the midway point between Seattle and Tacoma, where there is a steady parade of passing ships. There was always a waiting list for the station which had good fishing, hunting and lovely forest trails.

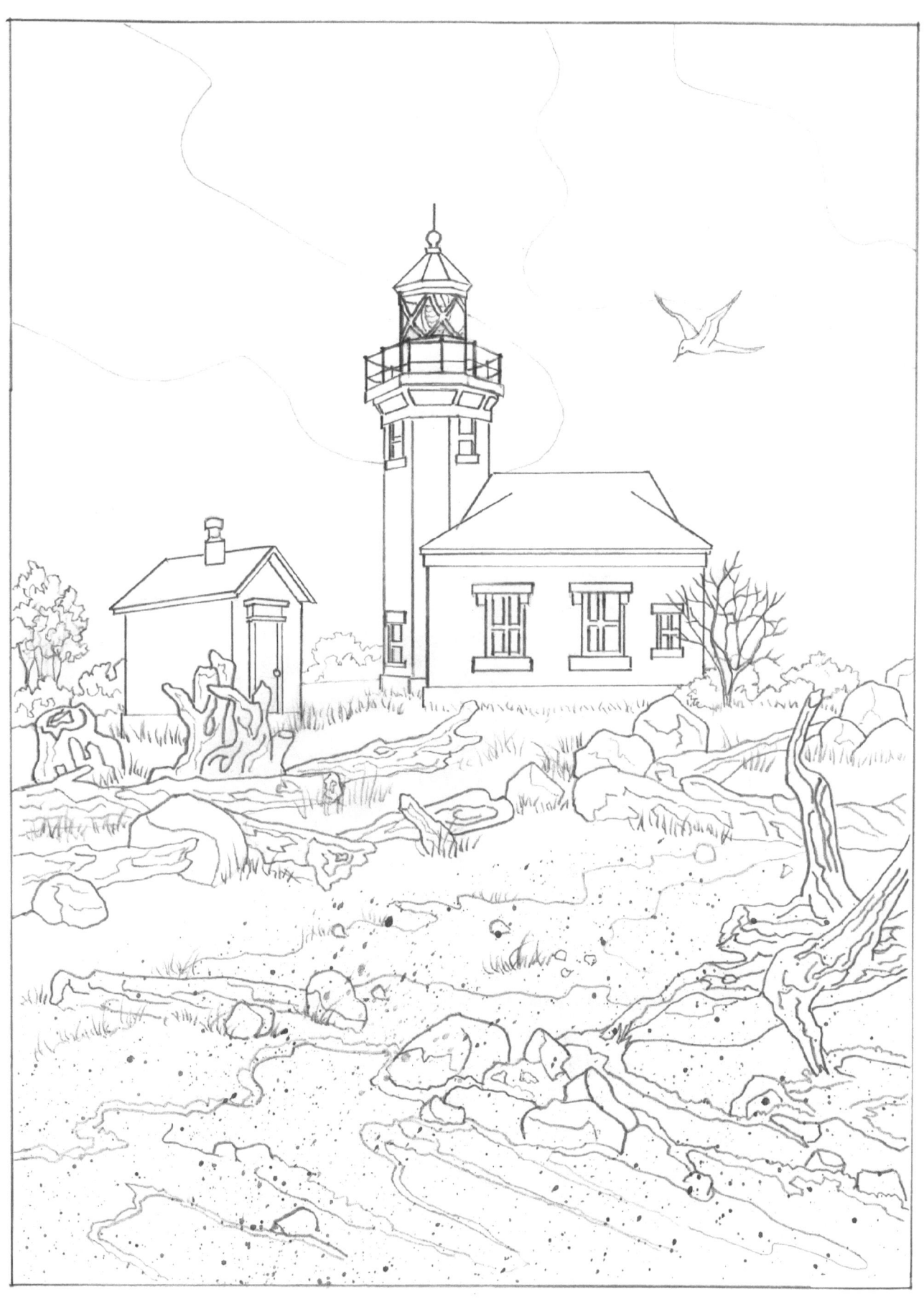

POINT ROBINSON - Maury Island, WA

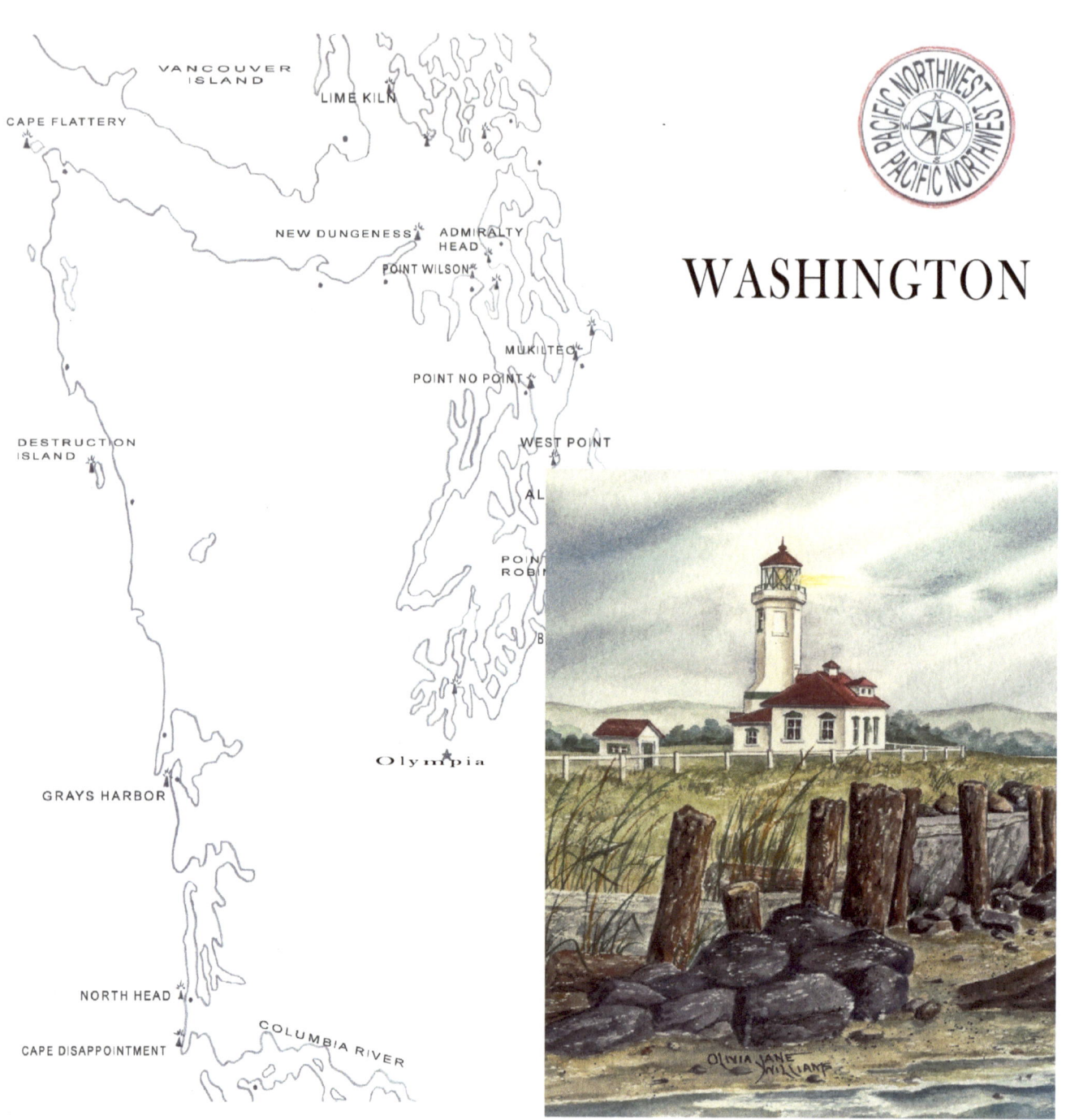

WASHINGTON

POINT WILSON LIGHTHOUSE, located in Fort Warden State Park near Port Townsend, was completed and lighted in 1914, replacing the original structure, which was threatened by high tides and erosion. Constructed of reinforced concrete, the forty-six foot octagonal tower was designed to reduce wind pressure on the building. The new lantern housed a fourth-order Fresnel lens that focused the light, visible from 270 degrees of horizon.

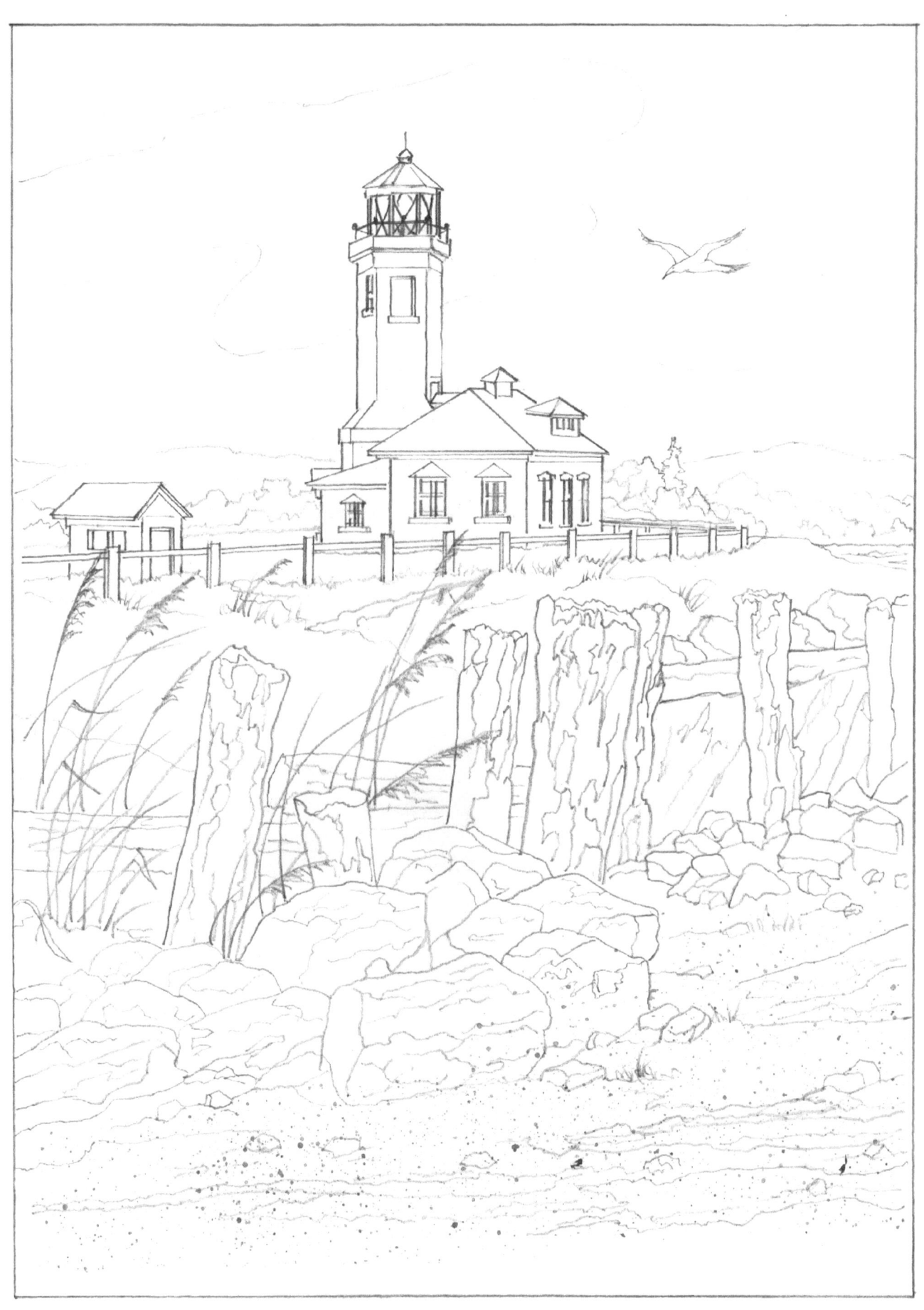

POINT WILSON - Port Townsend, WA

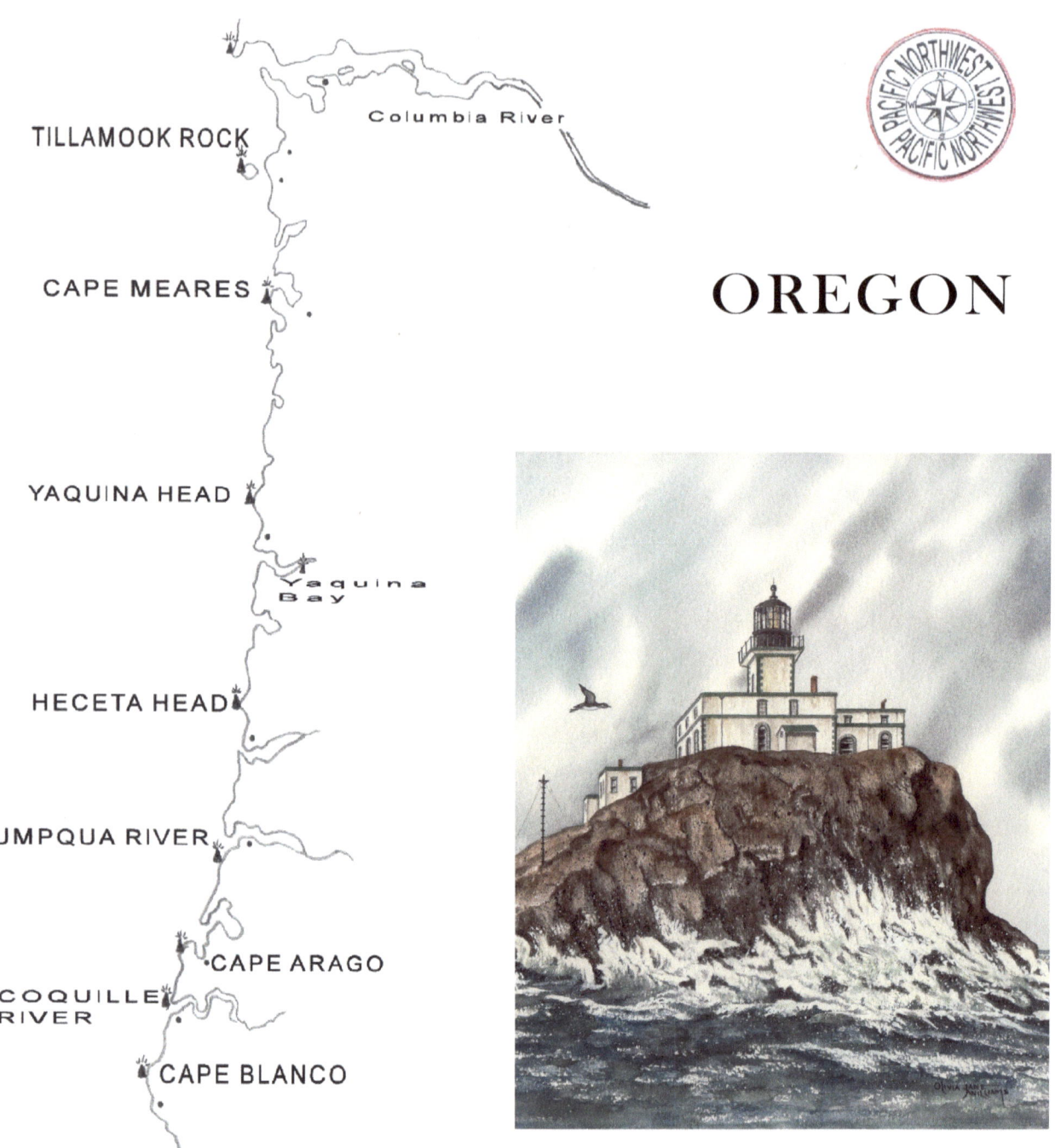

TILLAMOOK ROCK

Columbia River

CAPE MEARES

OREGON

YAQUINA HEAD

Yaquina Bay

HECETA HEAD

UMPQUA RIVER

CAPE ARAGO

COQUILLE RIVER

CAPE BLANCO

TILLAMOOK ROCK LIGHTHOUSE, located 20 miles south of the Columbia River and more than a mile off shore, was completed in 1881. Construction of the lighthouse was considered an engineering fete and many lives were lost during its' building.

The stone structure was fitted with a first-order Fresnel lens that shined almost continuously for seventy-six years. In 1957, the light was extinguished when the lighthouse was replaced by a buoy. The building now serves as a columbarium.

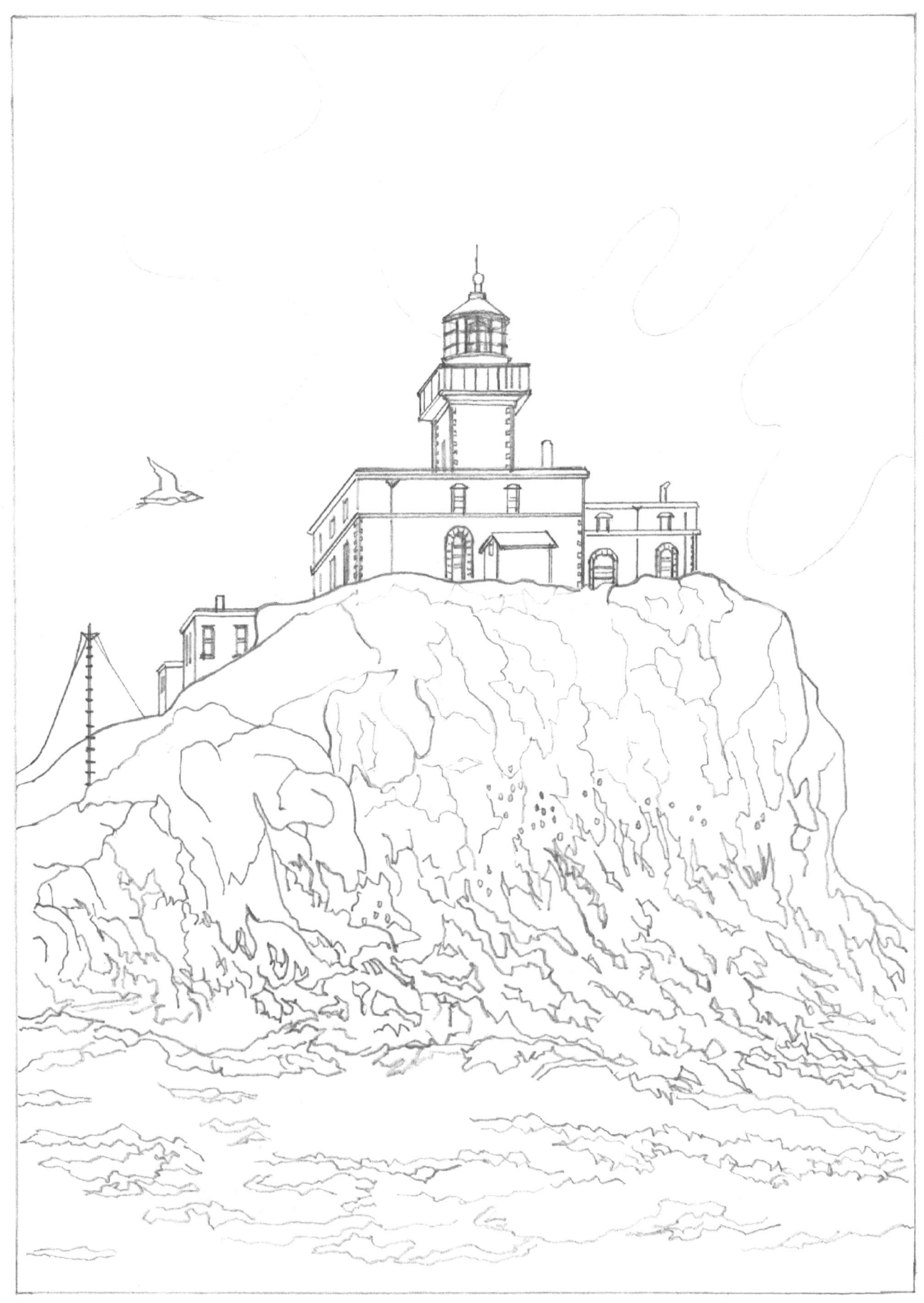

TILLAMOOK ROCK - Oregon

TILLAMOOK ROCK

Columbia River

CAPE MEARES

OREGON

YAQUINA HEAD

Yaquina
Bay

HECETA HEAD

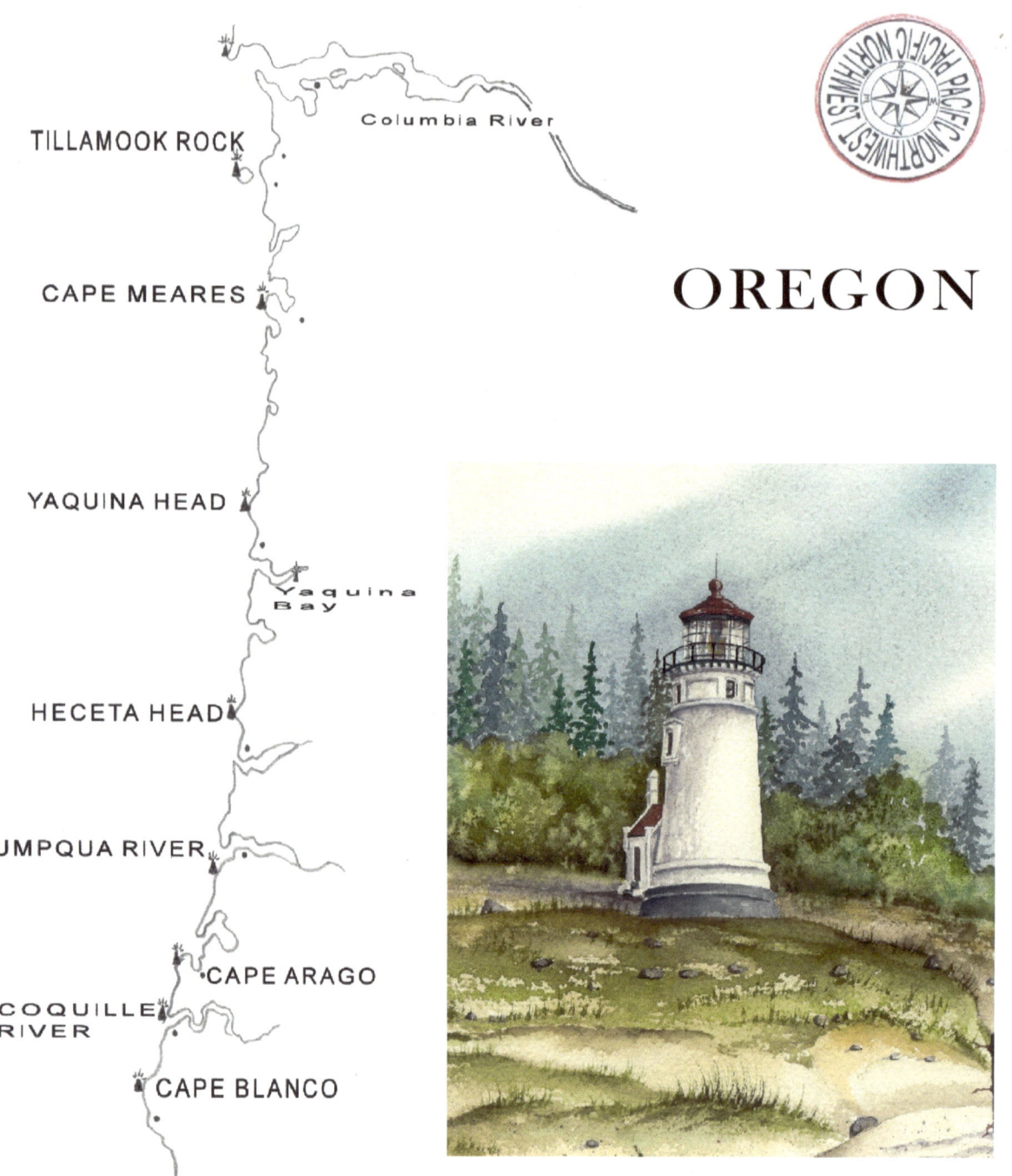

UMPQUA RIVER

CAPE ARAGO

COQUILLE
RIVER

CAPE BLANCO

UMPQUA RIVER LIGHTHOUSE, erected in 1894, guards the river's treacherous bar. Located south of Reedsport, it replaced Oregon's first tower, built in 1857. The elegant, sixty-five foot white tower, surrounded by tall evergreens and sand dunes, houses a first-order Fresnel lens that radiates light in rainbow brilliance over Winchester Bay.

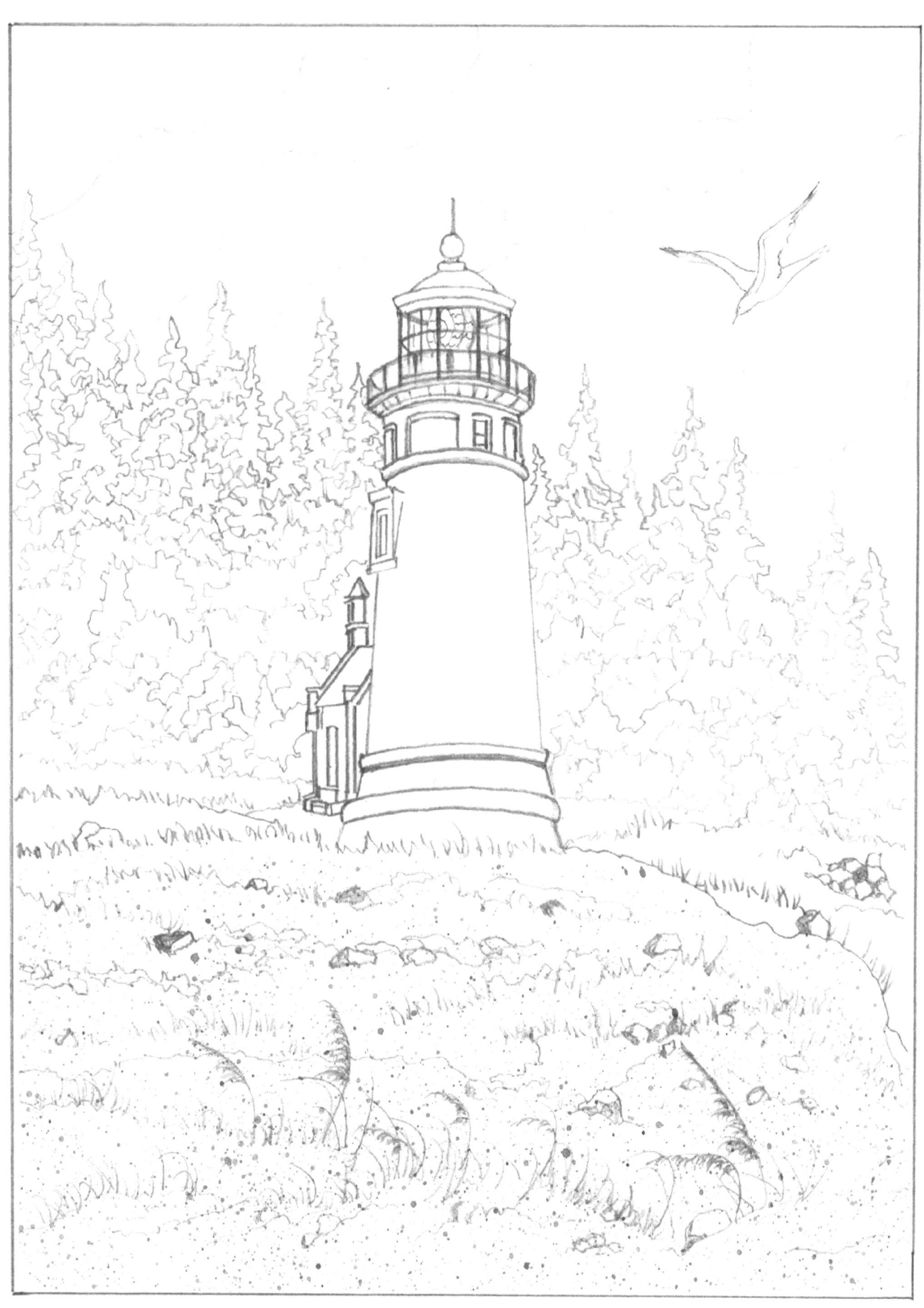

UMPQUA RIVER - Reedsport, OR

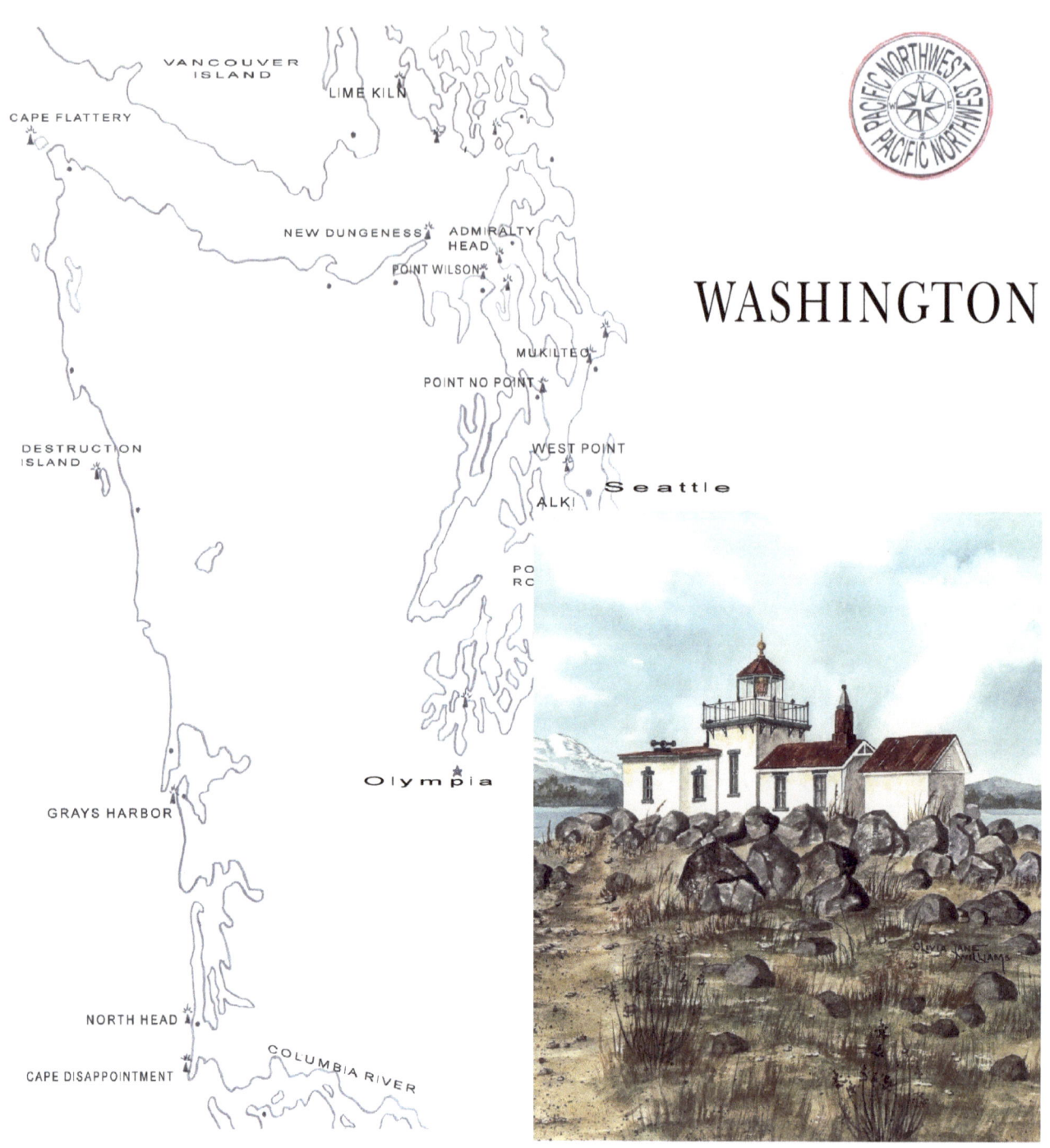

WASHINGTON

VANCOUVER
ISLAND

LIME KILN

CAPE FLATTERY

NEW DUNGENESS
ADMIRALTY
HEAD
POINT WILSON

MUKILTEO

POINT NO POINT

DESTRUCTION
ISLAND

WEST POINT

Seattle

ALKI

PO
RC

Olympia

GRAYS HARBOR

NORTH HEAD

COLUMBIA RIVER

CAPE DISAPPOINTMENT

WEST POINT LIGHTHOUSE, a landmark since November 1881, sits at the north entrance to Seattle's Elliott Bay at the foot of Magnolia Bluff in Discovery Park. The masonry tower stands only twenty-three feet and houses a fourth-order Frenel lens. It's white beam is visible fifteen miles away. Countless vessels pass the sentinel daily and it is considered Seattle's welcoming light.

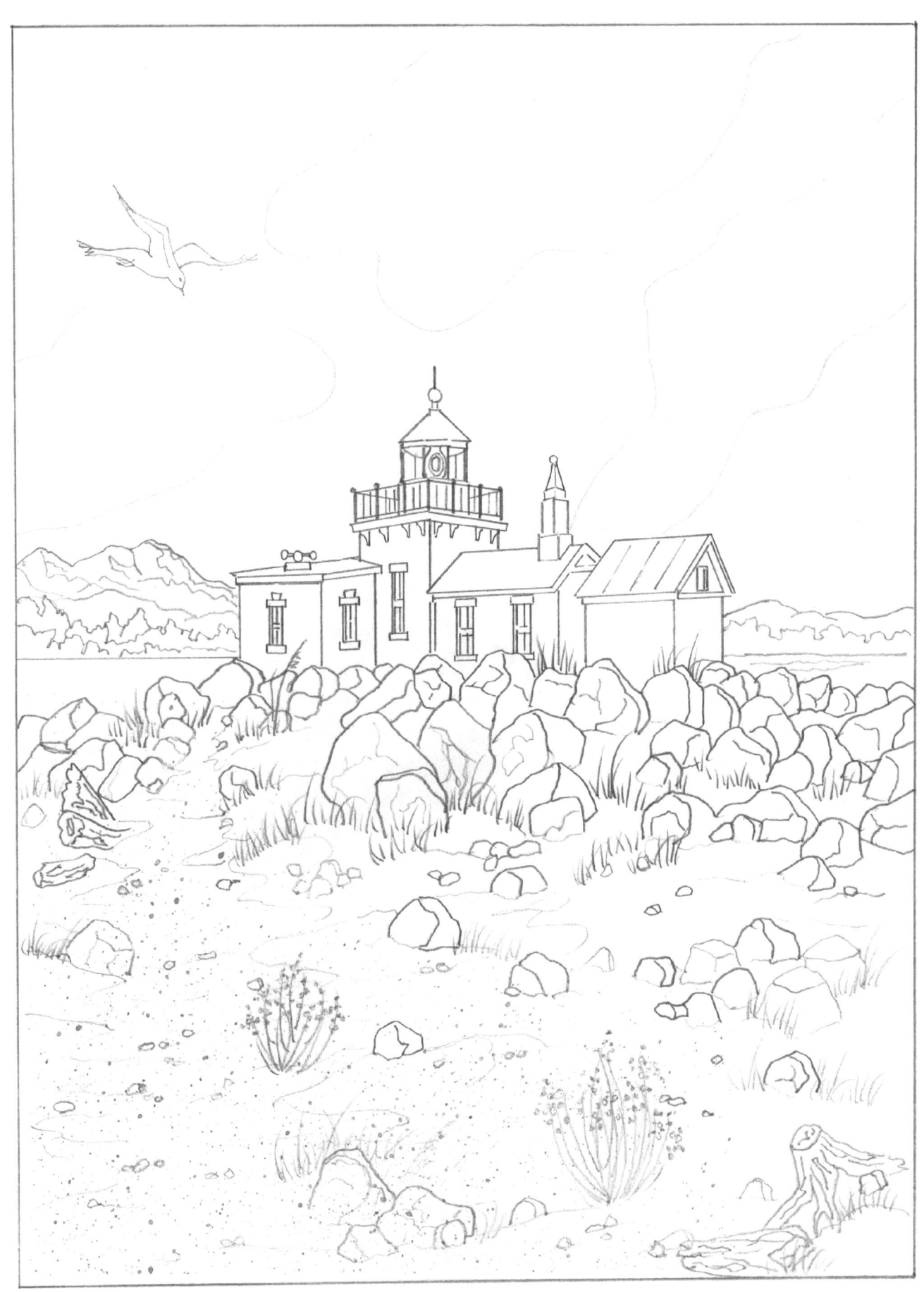

WEST POINT - Seattle, WA

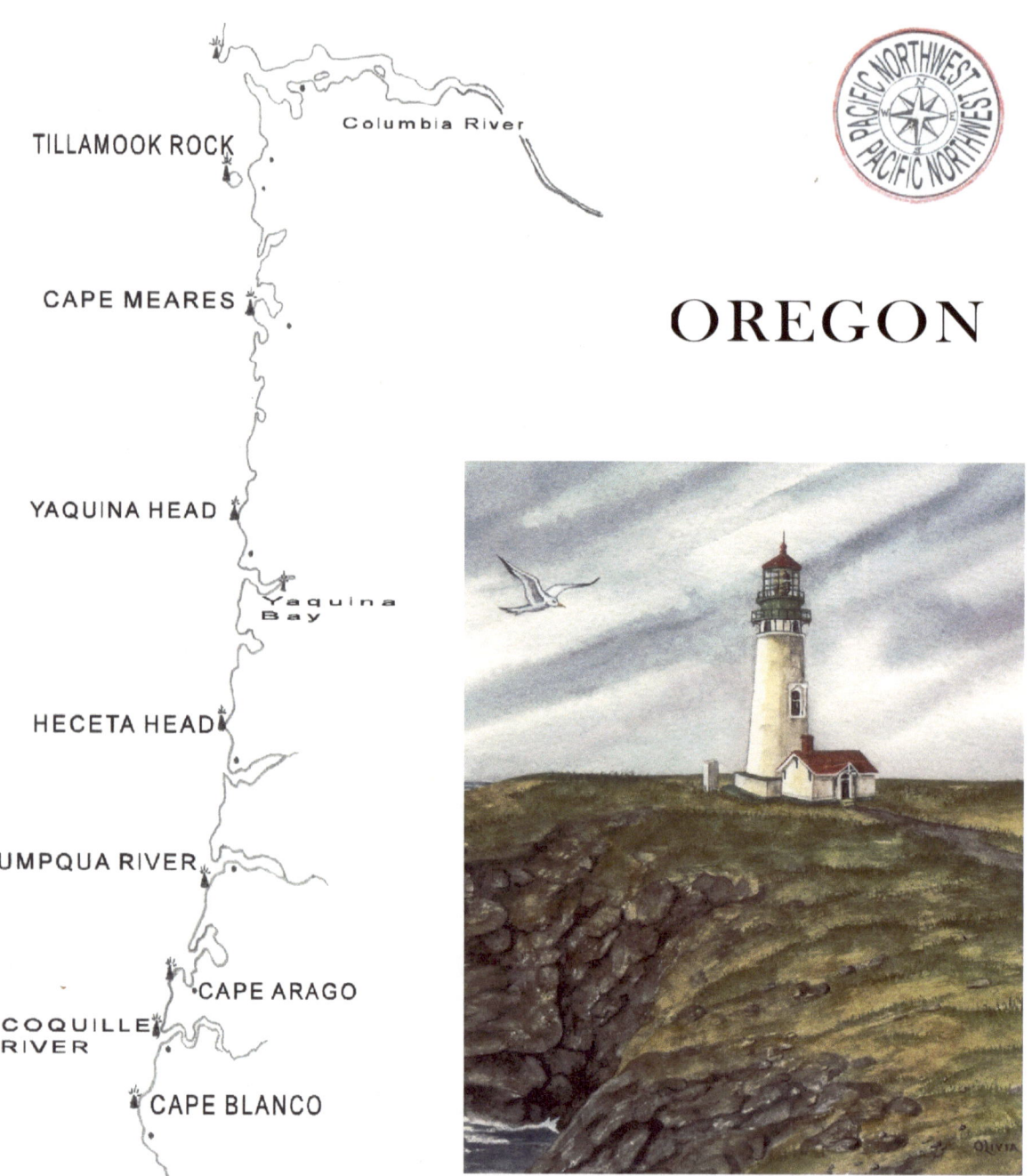

TILLAMOOK ROCK

Columbia River

CAPE MEARES

OREGON

YAQUINA HEAD

Yaquina Bay

HECETA HEAD

UMPQUA RIVER

CAPE ARAGO

COQUILLE RIVER

CAPE BLANCO

YAQUINA HEAD LIGHTHOUSE, located north of Newport, completed in 1873, sits on a core of magnatized iron that affects compasses of ships nearby. The ninety-three feet masonry tower is equipped with a first-order Fresnel lens that casts a beam visible nineteen miles at sea. The lighthouse is a favorite of photographers and tourists alike.

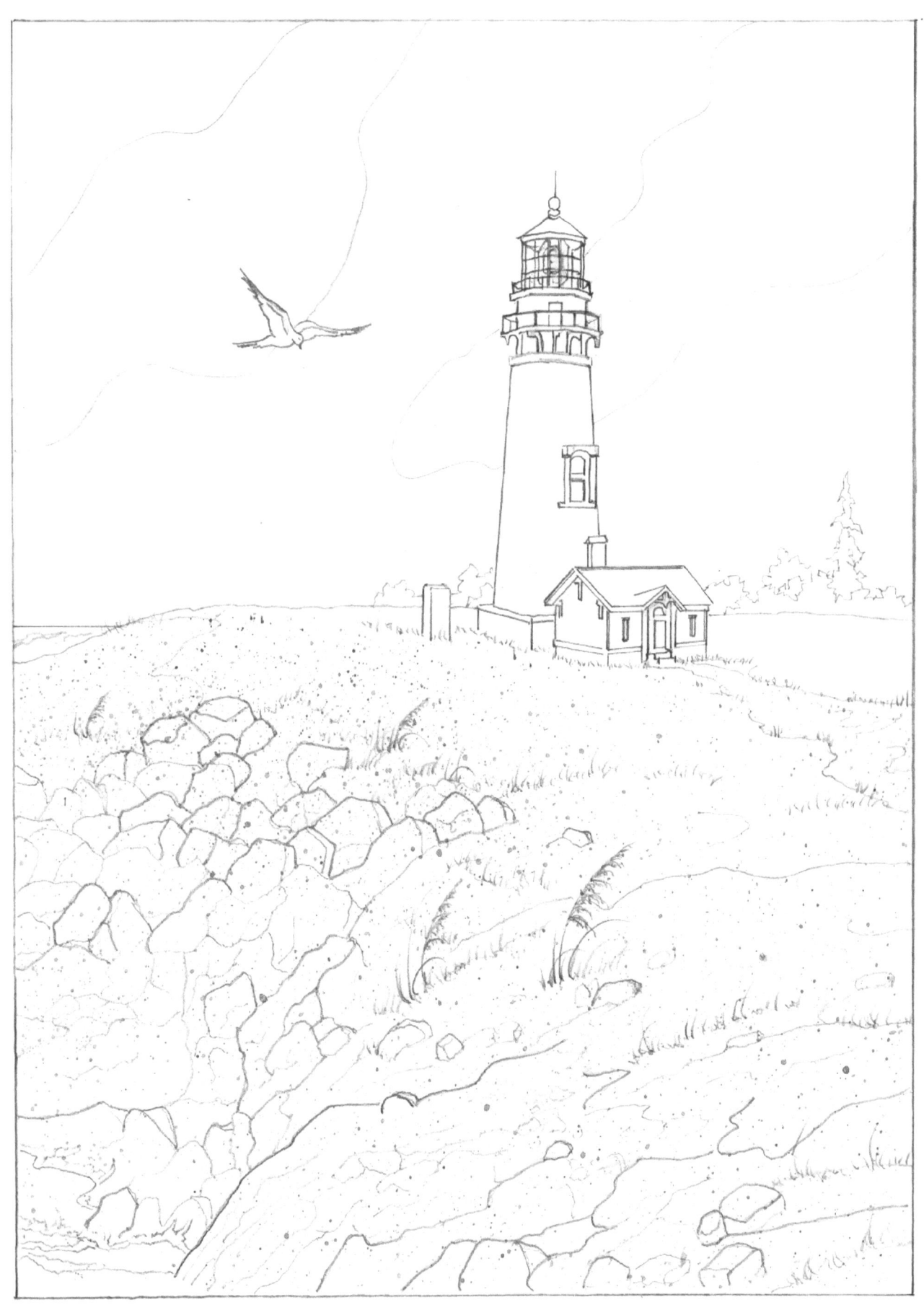

YAQUINA HEAD - Newport, OR

also available are all the lighthouses featured in this book matted in standard frame sizes and signed by the artist..................

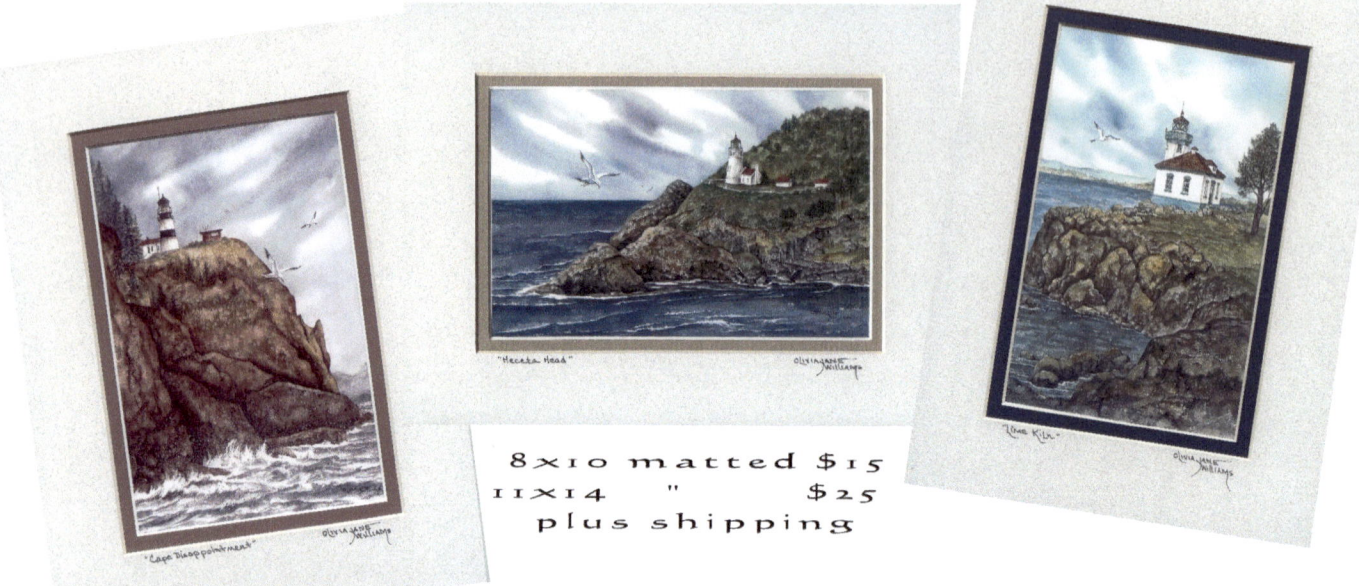

8x10 matted $15
11x14 " $25
plus shipping

and ....a special feature is the print remarqued in watercolor by the artist, which gives it a dimensional effect.

the beautiful LIGHTHOUSE MAP contains all the images and their locations............

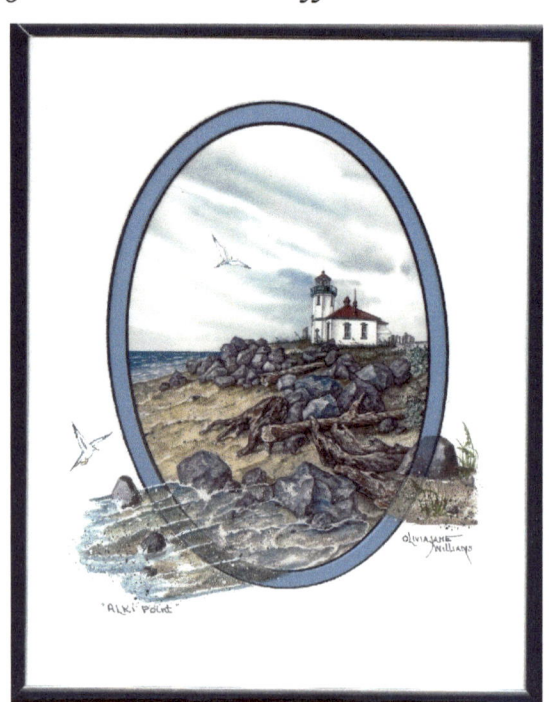

remarqued print
8x10 $25
11x14 $40
plus postage

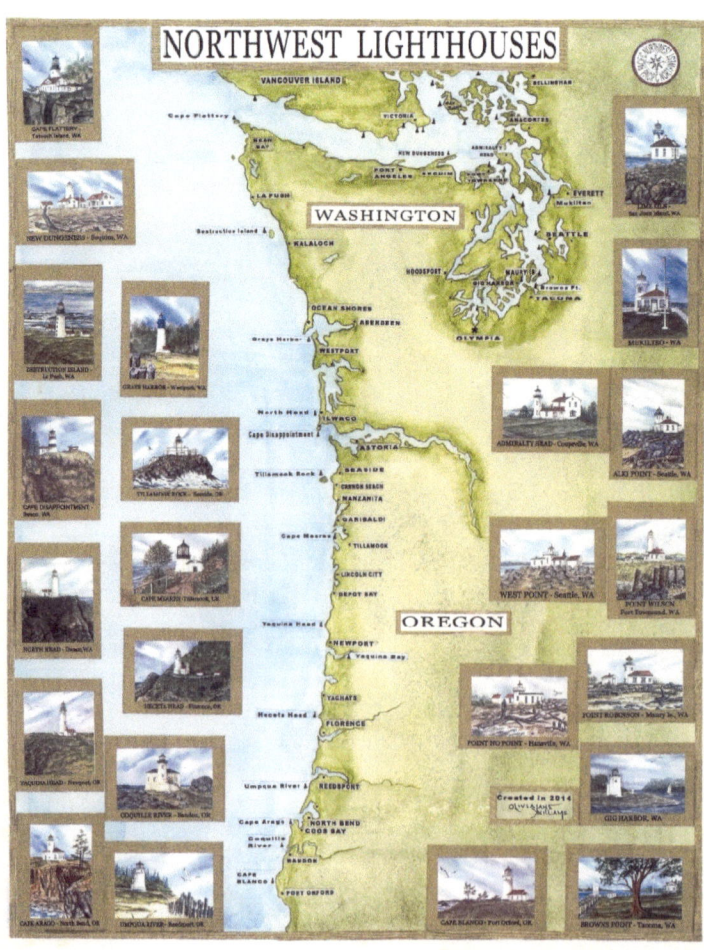

See these images and more on my website at ......www.oliviajanewilliams.com

Map 8x10 $10   11x14 $20
plus postage

www.ingramcontent.com/pod-product-compliance
Lightning Source LLC
Chambersburg PA
CBHW040746200526
45159CB00023B/1750